LEADERSHIP
FOR AN AGE OF
HIGHER CONSCIOUSNESS
VOLUME 2

ANCIENT WISDOM
FOR MODERN TIMES

B.T. SWAMI

WHAT OTHERS ARE SAYING ABOUT LEADERSHIP FOR AN AGE OF HIGHER CONSCIOUSNESS 2

"B.T. Swami is my dearest friend, brother and inspiration. Over thirty years, I closely witnessed in him a truly brilliant leader. Compassion was the principle of his life. He genuinely cares.

His devoted studies and his lifetime of service has inspired penetrating insight and profound wisdom that transcends all political, racial or sectarian barriers. His message is accessible, practical and non-judgmental.

During his life, B.T. Swami guided people of multi backgrounds, from university students to villagers in Africa, from corporate heads to the inner city downtrodden. He was a friend and guide to many world leaders including Nelson Mandela and Muhammed Ali.

In Leadership for an Age of Higher Consciousness B.T. Swami invites us to enter into the realm of empowered conscious leadership. He challenges us to go beneath the surface and recognize the authentic needs of those we lead.

His insights set the bar high, demonstrating why leadership is essential, how to be an empowered leader, and the powerful legacy this creates, both in the world and within the hearts of those we lead.

Please open your hearts to this treasure chest of wisdom. Let us raise ourselves and the world around us towards a higher level of consciousness, peace and compassion."

His Holiness Radhanatha Swami
Spiritual Guide, Author and Activist

"His Holiness B.T. Swami is one of those rare individuals who truly understands the essence of leadership. I have been greatly impressed by his humility and enthusiasm. He has had a major influence on world leaders from the political arena to the business community.

With the events of September 11, 2001 greatly impacting people's lives, B.T. Swami's weaving of spirituality, service and leadership into one cocoon is extremely timely. His message is truly profound and universal."

Peter Burwash
Author of The Key to Great Leadership
Leadership Coach, President & CEO of P.B.I.

"As much as his words inform, his example of living according to the highest standards of the Vedic tradition and in a constant attitude of listening for the divine guidance convey even more. Thus, you will feel a long-abiding faith in his words, as well as wisdom, and perhaps even the personal purity that allows him to raise the bar of leadership to truly spiritual heights. It is from such heights that visionary leadership is able to see the greatest expanse of human nature and its potentials, to guide it, not just for the upcoming fiscal year, but for generations into the future.

In focusing upon "higher consciousness," His Holiness B.T. Swami offers us a vision beyond materialistic competitiveness into the spiritual wholeness of existence. Thus, organizations following these ways can get beyond the harsh and limited modes of competitive functioning into the highly rewarding synergies of ever-greater cooperation and even world-embracing productivity and love. Here the bottom-line ascends to spiritual heights. Here, truly, awaits the best possible future for our newly emerging global marketplace and world culture, if we can find leaders capable of implementing such a vision."

Professor Stuart Sovatsky
Author of Words From the Soul: Time, East/West
Spirituality and the Psychotherapeutic Narrative
Clinical Supervisor, John F. Kennedy University

"Rather than being truly value-based organizations, too many firms today are toxic to the human spirit. Such management causes lack of synergy, lack of loyalty, demotivation and alienation. His Holiness B.T. Swami, in routinely traveling to dozens of countries each year giving seminars and workshops is surely doing his part in the international arena to help leaders and organizations become more hospitable to the human spirit. He is a personal mentor of mine and I am always glad when he is back in the U.S. to speak with my colleagues and to share his new books."

Armentha Cruise
President & CEO, Aspen Group
Chair, Women in Business, D.C. Chamber of Commerce
Leadership Board Member, Harvard University

"Over the years one of the most powerful things I have taken away from being a student in His Holiness B.T. Swami's classroom has been his passionate belief in living one's life and leading others from a position of love. His profound, inspiring and simple direction of living and working each day from a position of love, from a higher spiritual consciousness has been a powerful beam of light guiding me in my daily life and influencing how I try to teach others to lead. I have always believed and taught that great leaders are simply tool-givers—they provide the tools for others to be successful. *Leadership for an Age of Higher Consciousness, Volume II* is one of the tools that we can use to succeed as genuine leaders. B.T. Swami is a fantastic tool-giver! The ancient sages of India would be proud of his work and how he has captured their thoughts and lessons for the modern leader."

Ron Yudd
Former Director of Food Services for the U.S. Senate
International Leadership Consultant and trainer
Founding Director of Leadership Cares Foundation

"His Holiness B.T. Swami, whether appearing on television, giving seminars and workshops to national and international organizations, or meeting with diplomats and presidents of countries, his message is always profound and universal. He wants us to know that the greatest problems in the world are due to a crisis in leadership and we all can do something about it. This book is most timely now, while there is a rising interest in principle-centered leadership, servant-leadership and bringing spirituality into the workplace. I want to encourage the Swami to keep offering such wisdom to the international community, but most importantly I want to encourage those who want to lead with higher consciousness to devour this book."

Emerson Graham, M.D.
CEO, International Committee for U.S.D.

"On several occasions going back to the 1980's I was invited by one of our Directors, Pierre Adossama, to sit in as His Holiness B.T. Swami shared his insights on world-order problems with me and some of my colleagues at the U.N. in Geneva. On one return visit, after he had met with the President of Zambia (who was then the Chairman of the O.A.U.), and the Presidents of Botswana, Sierre Leone, Liberia and Ghana, it became clear in my mind how he expertly lives what he writes in all his books. As you study and apply his teaching in his *Leadership for an Age of Higher Consciousness* volumes you will also be given the tools to play your part in raising global consciousness."

Gabriel Mesfin
Labor Relations, International Labor Organization,
United Nations, Geneva, Switzerland

Copyright © 2002 by John E. Favors

All rights reserved. No part of this book may be reproduced, stored in a retrieval system, or transmitted in any form, by any means, including mechanical, electronic, photocopying, recording, or otherwise, without prior written consent of the publisher.

ISBN: 979-8-644076-91-8

First printing 2002

Second edition: Amazon KDP 2021

For information contact:

Hari-Nama Press

admin@harinamapress.org

◎ : bhaktitirthaswami

www.bhaktitirthaswami.com

TABLE OF CONTENTS

DEDICATION	1
THE MASTER AS SERVANT	3
PREFACE	9
ACKNOWLEDGMENTS	13
INTRODUCTION	15

PART I THE INSTRUCTIONS OF BHISHMADEVA

WHY GOOD LEADERSHIP IS ESSENTIAL	22
SYSTEMS OF GOVERNMENT	23
THE VALUE OF A DIVINELY INSPIRED MONARCH	28
THE IMPORTANCE OF SPEAKER AND HEARER	29
WHY IS A KING NECESSARY?	31
A LEADER'S FIRST CONQUEST	32
BHISHMADEVA'S QUALIFICATIONS	33

A COMPLEX SCIENCE	36
THE KING'S DUTY IS SPIRITUAL	39
A TRUE LEADER IS ABOVE DUPLICITY	43
THE OPULENCE OF POWER	44
SACRED POWER, DIVINE POWER	47
GOOD LEADERSHIP IS BALANCED	49
A LEADER MUST BE COMPASSIONATE BUT STRONG	54
A LEADER MUST KNOW FRIEND AND FOE ALIKE	57
CONSIDERING ONE'S PEOPLE BEFORE ONESELF	58
PARENTAL SPIRIT	58
INDEPENDENCE	59
THE FEAR OF THE FACELESS	59
RECOGNIZING ONE'S OWN WEAKNESS	60
CONTROLLING ONE'S DESIRES	61
TRUTH AND WEALTH	61
THE WISDOM OF AGE	62
HARBOR NO MALICE	63
THE IMPORTANCE OF ALLIANCES	64
AN IMPRESSIVE IMPRESSION	70
BE PREPARED FOR EVERYTHING	71
ALL THE KING'S MEN	71
BE DIRECTLY INVOLVED	72

UNDERSTANDING THE PRINCIPLE OF SELF-INTEREST	72
APPROPRIATE PUNISHMENT	73
ENVIRONMENTAL CONCERNS	73
PARENTAL MOOD REVISITED	74
GOOD ASSOCIATION	75
NICE WORDS	76
THE IMPORTANCE OF CHARACTER	77
VISIONARY LEADERSHIP	78
CONCLUSION	83

PART II SERVANT-LEADERSHIP: PAST AND PRESENT

QUESTIONS AND ANSWERS RELATED TO THE RULE OF KING PRITHU	87
LEADERS ARE BORN FROM THE PEOPLE	87
WHAT MAKES A LEADER?	88
HIGHLIGHTS OF A TRUE LEADER'S CHARACTER	91
TEN CHARACTERISTICS OF A SERVANT-LEADER	92
FINDING COMMON GROUND	121
QUALITIES OF DIVINE MONARCHS	123
ALTERNATIVE GOVERNMENTS FOR THE CURRENT AGE	127
PROTECTION FROM THIEVES AND CHEATERS	130
ACCOUNTABILITY OF A LEADER	135
PRINCIPLES AND PRACTICES OF JUSTICE	138

CRIMINAL JUSTICE IN MODERN SUPERPOWERS	145
WHEN THE KING MAKES MISTAKES	147
THE CITIZENS MUST PERFORM THEIR DUTIES	151
PROMOTING INTERDEPENDENCE	154
WHERE DOES A LEADER'S RESPONSIBILITY BEGIN AND END?	156
DIFFICULTIES FROM FAMILY	160
WHEN LEADERS QUIT THEIR POSTS	161
WHEN LEADERS ARE TOO NICE	163
THE POWER OF AUSTERITY	165
BUILDING CHARACTER	170
CHARACTER IN COMMUNITY	175
GOALS AND A SENSE OF DUTY	178
DEVELOPING THE WORKFORCE	180
LEADERS NEED GUIDES	183
LEARN BY TEACHING	185
DEVELOPING GOOD GUIDES	188
THE FOUR SOCIAL CLASSES	191
CAN MODERN LEADERS PROTECT THE CITIZENS?	194
DEVELOPING GENUINE COMMUNITY	196
LEADERS MUST SOMETIMES BECOME ANGRY	197
KEEPING TOO MANY SECRETS	199
PRIDE & EGO	201

IMPLEMENTING VARNASRAMA-DHARMA	204
BEING RIGHT IN THE RIGHT WAY	206
BLIND FOLLOWING	209
DEALING WITH DEVIANTS	212
TRAINING PEOPLE TO RECOGNIZE GOOD LEADERSHIP	215
UNDERSTANDING POWER	217
GENUINE HUMILITY	220
EIGHT SINS OF LEADERSHIP	222
ADDRESS THE HIGHEST NEEDS	223
FINDING TRUTH	227
FINDING KNOWLEDGE	232
AVOID OVERDEPENDENCE	234
SPIRITUALITY IN THE WORKPLACE	234
CULTIVATING LOVE	237
THE MODE OF GOODNESS	241
MANIC LEADERS VS. SERVANT-LEADERS	243
LEADERS' PRIVATE & PUBLIC LIVES	245
DANGERS OF BLIND ENJOYMENT	250
OUR HIGHER PURPOSE	251
MATERIALISTIC GURUS	253
A CIVILIZATION IN DECLINE	254

CONCLUSIONS	259
EPILOGUE	263
GLOSSARY	267
BIBLIOGRAPHY	281
ABOUT THE AUTHOR	285
BOOKS FROM HARI-NAMA PRESS	289

DEDICATION

This book is a gift from my heart to the monarchs, heads-of-state and heads-of-households that I have had the opportunity to assist and learn from over the many years. May your strength and compassion light the way for an age of higher consciousness.

THE MASTER AS SERVANT

FOREWORD BY KEN SHELTON

One of the great "Spiritual Warriors" of our time, His Holiness Bhakti Tirtha Swami, has done it again! His new work on leadership—one of about 10,000 titles on leadership to be published in recent decades—sets a new standard, expressly because it explores the spiritual dimension in ways that popular *gurus* like Stephen R. Covey (*Principle-Centered Leadership*), Kevin Cashman (*Leadership from the Inside Out*), and Ken Blanchard (*Situational Leadership*) have not done.

While the topic of servant-leadership has certainly been explored before, most notably by Peter Block in *Servant Leadership* and by Robert Spitzer in *The Spirit of Leadership*, Swami plumbs the spiritual depths and the spiritual roots. "The true servant leader," he writes, "assesses the primary needs of his followers and compassionately serves them, having a profound understanding of the highest good beyond material requirements and servicing the soul, the real identity, of each and every individual."

His profound insights, largely based on ancient India's Vedic literature, will assist readers in their work life and their leadership of others. His principles have universal application. For example, by defining leadership in terms such as "actions that attract followers" and "standards set by exemplary acts" that others wish to pursue, Swami helps us see that leaders set examples and patterns for us to follow, whether those paths be in political, economic, academic or social realms. Indeed, in a world of tabloid heroes and skin-deep virtues, Swami provides us laser-accurate core values. He gets to the bedrock, the absolute essence of authentic leadership. This is a guidebook for personal and professional integrity, the most significant issue of the century.

In his revealing work, Swami examines various forms of what I call "counterfeit leadership," and shows how to detect authentic leadership. "The ability to recognize good leadership," he writes, "is almost as important as good leadership itself." Since not everyone recognizes great messengers when they appear in human form, Swami advocates teaching how to recognize great teachers and leaders "to distinguish the bona fide from the deviant."

Real leadership is often hard to detect because of the rules and biases built into social, academic, and professional systems. Hence, we are short on leadership, long on counterfeit. Our coffers are filled with pyrite, and our offices are filled with pirates.

In his book, Swami explores the characteristics of authentic leadership. He reveals that true leaders share at least 10 common traits:

1. They love people and are sensitive to their emotions and needs
2. They help people feel happy and secure
3. They create lasting value at all times
4. They are philosophers—they seek to convey ultimate abiding truth
5. They lead from the inside out, knowing that character is power
6. They are principle-centered
7. They are powerful visionaries
8. They keep everyone engaged according to their propensities
9. They are experts at delegation and empowerment
10. They are servant-leaders who leave behind a culture of enduring excellence.

This is not the Tom Peters brand of here-today, gone-tomorrow excellence. Having been in search of excellence all his life, Swami has found more than a few secrets. He notes: "Improper leadership causes imbalances and crises in the lives of people. Under proper leadership, people are showered with adequate food, health and wealth." On the other hand, when leaders are weak, people are weak. "It is then a matter of the blind leading the blind. Society becomes a venture of tremendous speculation, frustration, and diminishing returns."

Those of us who deposit time, trust, money, and other forms of investment in leaders and their organizations always like to see at least a modest return on our investment. For this reason, Swami also sees leadership from an accounting point of view, calculating ROI. He suggests that when people invest resources and energy in someone or something, they expect a proportionately valuable profit. The best leaders deliver.

On the issue of power, Swami sees both the upside, "Power is wonderful when used properly," and the downside: "But, when used improperly, power is a tremendous deficit. When leaders try to gather opulence unto themselves we have an unhealthy situation. In a society of people who manipulate others to gain power, people lose their focus on the soul."

Bottom line, says Swami, the leader of high conscience creates a culture that stimulates people to do the right thing in the right way and at the right time. That's his idea of "visionary" servant-leadership—providing spiritual leadership to heal the ills of a material society.

So, if you care about making a meaningful contribution with your life and work, I suggest you adopt Swami's principles of visionary servant-leadership and apply them to your situation. Should you choose to do so, I suspect that your leadership will take on a whole new dimension. People will take you seriously and want to follow you. They will gladly sign up to help make your vision of great good a reality for the benefit and blessing of many, perhaps millions, of God's children on earth. Sounds like the real deal—the spiritual warrior rides again!

Ken Shelton
Editor of Executive Excellence,
Author of Beyond Counterfeit Leadership

> *"What you are shouts so loud in my ears, I cannot hear what you say."*
>
> —Ralph Waldo Emerson

PREFACE

This book discusses leadership in a distinct way: It explains how to "be in charge," to rule, or to lead, with the mass of people in mind. The method presented in this book seeks to train leaders "as if people mattered." In short, it espouses "servant-leadership" — a phenomenon that allows a leader to see his or her identification with those whom they lead. It teaches how to be a servant and a leader at the same time.

While such concepts have been beaten into the ground, as it were, this book proposes something new, something that augments existing leadership techniques, even those that are progressive and "spiritual." Many prominent, principle-centered leaders are tired of talking or writing about spirituality in the workplace and now they want to see it more actualized. They want to move beyond outdated conceptions of servant-leadership, or empty slogans such as "managing as if people mattered," "empowering people in the workplace," etc.—these are well-intentioned first steps, but are still generally operating on old paradigms.

This is so because these systems of management normally still seek to use people for mundane results, or to satisfy the lesser goals of would-be managers and/or their dependents. Such CEOs and "leaders" of corporations may resemble actual servant-leaders as the term is commonly understood, but they are usually opportunistic businessmen who by good fortune or other endeavors managed to secure a position that they often do not deserve. In the same way that politicians often use God's name to bolster their efforts and to pursue their personal agenda—while actually having little or no interest in God consciousness—most contemporary leaders speak of progressive conceptions of leadership and spirituality merely to win adherents and supporters. Their primary concern is continually how to use people to make things happen rather than making things happen for the people.

Our discussion of servant-leadership goes beyond these superficial approaches. It is, however, extremely complex and broad-based, and unless one is serious about understanding it as it is, one would do well to put this book down right now. What you will read here includes expressions of servant-leadership on both elementary and mature platforms, from introductory concepts to subtle nuances of developed theory. Our basic thesis is that true (and mature) servant-leadership is impossible without embracing a deeply developed form of universal spirituality. This is so because the mature servant-leader is a natural philosopher and spiritualist; these highly evolved components are as fundamental to his or her way of being as food is to any other living organism.

A true servant-leader assesses the primary needs of his dependents and compassionately serves them. For this to occur, the servant-leader must have a profound understanding of the highest good, which necessarily goes beyond mere material requirements. Ultimately, a servant-leader focuses on our identity as spiritual beings, as people who undergo material experiences even though, at their very core, they are beyond matter. Thus, the mature servant-leader must assist in servicing the soul, the real identity of each and every individual. It is the soul that is the highest expression of humanity and mature servant-leadership has little meaning without recognition of this.

As a final note, it should be pointed out that many of the insights in this book are based on ancient India's Vedic literature, particularly the *Srimad-Bhagavatam* and the *Mahabharata*. The story of Grandfather Bhishmadeva, as found in the pages of these holy books, is especially replete with details on the importance of servant-leadership. Moreover, the minutiae of spiritual government are nowhere as developed as in these ancient texts, which analyze the perfection of a ruling class in terms of theological science. It is not necessary for readers of this work to familiarize themselves with these ancient Indian texts. The present book sifts through the essential teachings of ancient India's sages, and offers our readers a summarization of all its teachings in relation to the subject at hand. However, when one comes across unfamiliar terms and personalities, the reader should consult the glossary for assistance. Throughout the book, please keep in mind that when we refer to Krishna, we are referring to the same one God with whom we are familiar. And the term Vaisnava refers to those who worship God according to these ancient traditions. Armed with these elementary words and concepts, we are prepared to delve into our first lessons in mature servant-leadership as derived from the Vedic literature.

ACKNOWLEDGMENTS

I would like to thank Stewart Cannon, Michael Buhler-Rose and Christine Kenney for their hard work on the cover design and publishing. I would also like to thank Kathryn Ballach, Steven J. Rosen, Lauren Holloway, Jason Gerick, Krista Oliver and Adam Kenney for their careful editing of the text. Thanks also to the many members of our staff who transcribed numerous audiotapes, and to a wonderful group of my students in New York who assisted financially with the printing. Special thanks to Kathryn Ballach, Gilda Dixon and James Parks who presented the questions for Part II.

INTRODUCTION

This book focuses on the subject of leadership by using the proven methods of the Vaisnava ruling class in ancient India. These teachings have universal application and are not confined to the geographical location that gave them birth. We specifically look at the great warrior-mystic Bhishmadeva's instructions to Yudhisthira, as well as at insights from the life of the great Prithu Maharaja, a renowned king described in the ancient classic, *Srimad-Bhagavatam*.

Before delving into specifics, however, we would first like to look at the general idea of leadership and how it has been viewed in modern times. As a beginning point, let us appreciate that everything a person does has some kind of "leadership" component, either directly or indirectly. This can be seen in the simple fact that every act invariably influences someone in some way. The *Bhagavad-gita*, which is part of the *Mahabharata*, clearly says:

> "Whatever action a great man performs, common men follow. And whatever standards he sets by exemplary acts, all the world pursues."
>
> —Bhagavad-gita, 3.21

This is true in all arenas, whether political, economic, academic or social. Leaders help form our worldview. They set patterns for us to follow. Sometimes they impose those patterns upon us. Even if we reject a given leader's patterns, we might still find ourselves emulating them. For example, the United States is a world leader, and even though there are countries that hate American policy and culture, so many of them base their own policies on those found in America. Therefore, one way to examine world history and civilization is to study its leaders, the policies they set in motion, the examples they project, and what the people in general follow or rebel against. In this way, all world concerns and crises have something to do with leadership.

We may wonder, if leadership is such a strong force behind almost everything we do, why does society suffer, even in the face of good leadership? We see that when the Lord and great prophets appear, societies are still beset by difficulties. In a world where things are by nature temporary and limited, obstacles are par for the course, an inevitability that must be accepted as part of life. When deeply contemplating the world in which we live, it seems as though "difficulty" is synonymous with "existence." It is a simple statement of fact that a true leader does not deny the limitations and drawbacks of the material world, and in fact uses these to help others come to a higher level.

It is also true that the ability to recognize good leadership is almost as important as good leadership itself. Not everyone recognizes the incarnations or great messengers when they appear in human form. We must be taught how to recognize incarnations, *gurus*, teachers, and great leaders. There must be systems of being able to distinguish the bona fide from the deviant. In fact, good leadership entails making such distinctions and teaching others how to do the same.

There is a story in the *Srimad-Bhagavatam* that illustrates the faith citizens once placed in proper leadership, and how good leaders were gauged by how well their citizens fared in their day-to-day lives. Once, in the ancient city of Dvaraka, a priest's wife gave birth to a son, who immediately died. The father took his dead baby to King Ugrasena's court, berating the king for the untimely death of his son. The priest told King Ugrasena that he must be directly responsible for his child's death, because the untimely death of a child was unheard of in a kingdom where the king was properly executing his duty. Obviously, this was a time much unlike our own: Not only did people have extremely high expectations of a good ruler, but the ruler was able to fulfill every need of his faithful constituency.

Before going further, let us pause and consider some universal characteristics of authentic leaders:

1. They love people and are sensitive to their emotions and needs
2. They help people feel happy and secure
3. They create lasting value at all times
4. They are philosophers—they seek to convey ultimate abiding truth
5. They lead from the inside out, knowing that character is power
6. They are principle-centered
7. They are powerful visionaries
8. They keep everyone engaged according to their propensities
9. They are experts at delegation and empowerment
10. They are servant-leaders who leave behind a culture of enduring excellence.

Improper leadership causes imbalances and crises in the lives of the citizens. Under proper leadership, however, the demigods reciprocate by showering the people on earth with food, health and wealth. In ancient cultures, particularly Vedic culture, it was recognized that higher powers were pleased when good leadership reigned. Even in post-modern society, it is acknowledged by progressive thinkers that the environment virtually rejoices when leadership is good, and that the world is generally a better place. This correlates with the idea that demigods are pleased when witnessing the work of a good leader.

Good quality leadership and the people's ability to recognize this quality in their leaders are important. When both are present, society flourishes. Such conditions were present hundreds of thousands of years ago in Satya-yuga, the age of great piety. There were both powerfully qualified leaders and citizens equally qualified to support them—and to recognize when leaders were no longer performing their duties properly. Thus, it is said that "the leaders make the people and the people make the leaders." As the people's collective consciousness becomes elevated, they will naturally produce more elevated leaders from among them; as the leaders' consciousness becomes elevated, they will support a more elevated citizenry. When the leaders are weak, the people are weak. When this is the case, it is a matter of the blind leading the blind. Society becomes a venture of tremendous speculation, frustration, and diminishing returns.

PART I
THE INSTRUCTIONS OF BHISHMADEVA

> *"We are what we repeatedly do. Hence the power to control our actions is the power to control our character, and the power to control our character is the power to control our lives."*
>
> -**Aristotle**

WHY GOOD LEADERSHIP IS ESSENTIAL

"Diminishing returns" happen when resources are invested in something that fails to turn a proportionately valuable profit. That is, the returns become less over time, and remain minimal or superficial. There are different types of governments or leadership systems, all of which are meant to maintain, organize and oversee others. Each of these systems makes a significant impact on how the people working under them interact, grow and achieve purpose in their lives. When leadership has no higher understanding, people in general become bewildered. The masses of people are basically subordinate by nature. Many great secular philosophers have understood this quality in most people. Voltaire surmised that because the masses are willingly subordinate, they tend to follow fads and whatever society deems normal at any given time.

We understand from the Vedic scriptures that the healthiest system of government is divine monarchy. In the material world, it is the system that God Himself recommends. However, a monarchy is the most easily abused system of all, and when wrongly applied, it can become a source of social devastation. When those with a demoniac mentality rule, they create great disturbances by misusing their power. Consequently, although divine monarchy—properly executed—can offer the highest benefits to the people, it is presently more of an idea than a reality. Other systems of government, therefore, may work better for the current times, and some of these will now be considered. But remember that these are second best: A divine monarchy, when led by a person who is actually qualified, will bestow the greatest benefits on those who live under its shelter.

SYSTEMS OF GOVERNMENT

Socialism is a system that allows for the means of production and distribution to be owned and controlled collectively. In theory, socialism is meant to lead to communism, a doctrine that allows for all property to be owned and controlled by "the community." A communist society is ideally classless, but in the communist societies we have seen in recent history, the state is controlled by a totalitarian regime. They have been atheistic, and the totalitarian government has imposed its policies upon the people, "for their own good," with no room for differences.

Another government system is dictatorship. A dictator will inevitably exploit the people to ensure his or her own power. Those who do not accept the dictator's rule are punished. People are literally forced to accept the dictator's policies. History has shown that dictators are often egomaniacal, with little concern for anything beyond their own personal agendas. Under such a regime, people in general feel exploited and unhappy.

Then there is oligarchy, which means, "rule by a few." These few then select leaders from among themselves. For example, the masses do not select their leaders; rather, the members themselves have power of attorney to select their chairman, vice-chairman, treasurer, and other officers. Some organizations and communities look toward oligarchy as a viable way to run themselves, because they realize both the need for strong leadership and the possibility of exploitative leadership. Oligarchy provides a community with the semblance of a monarch, although after a certain time, the power rotates to another leader in their governing system. This system allows communities to minimize the possibility of dictatorship by setting in place a more thorough monitoring system.

There is also democracy. In some respects, democracy is the most dangerous system of all. In a communistic government, at least, there is only one direction in which the society can go—the direction chosen by the totalitarian government. Under a totalitarian regime, both policies and the citizens' roles are clearly defined. There is no ambiguity about goals or direction.

Life under a democratic government, however, is more vague. Democracy is defined as a "government for the people and by the people," but such a government is actually impossible to achieve under this system. Democracy is based on which party or group has the greater influence, which can mean that the group with the most money to spend on advertising will generally win. Democracy doesn't really bring equality to the citizens, although it pretends to.

Democracy has been referred to as "demon-crazy." That is because there is an inherent and essential flaw in its methods—reality is not dictated by majority vote. That is, simply because the majority agree on a particular course of action, does not make that action the proper way to go. For example, if a group of children were to vote on how many days per week they wished to attend school, there would be few school days in a year. Similarly, when the people tend to be both of mundane quality and misinformed about the goal of life, they will agree on a substandard and irreligious lifestyle and cause disturbance in society. Clearly, popular vote is not the best way to discern right from wrong.

There is another type of democracy that many New Age people are investigating in their attempt to develop communities: The idea of total consensus. This style of leadership is also dangerous. To reach total consensus requires continuous discussion and processing until everyone agrees. The end result looks as if everyone is satisfied, but this is really not the case. By the time total consensus is reached, many people have become tired and have given up on the issues at hand. Most of them settle for almost any resolution just so they can move on to other pursuits. Therefore, many unhealthy compromises take place, most of which do not guarantee the greatest good for all concerned. The decision of unanimous choice ends up being whatever people are finally ready to accept. We often find this model in communities that are trying to create a sense of concern for every member, but without an understanding of higher principles, their attempts amount to little more than misplaced sentiment.

Many people feel that despite any disadvantages, democracy is still the fairest form of government. After all, democracy is based on the premise that all people are equal. But Vaisnavas and scholars of Vedic culture do not accept this premise. Even our physical traits point to the fact that we are unique, as Barbara Gray highlights in her book *Energy Management*:

1. Fingerprints. There is less than one chance in 64 billion that two fingerprints are the same.
2. No two faces are alike.
3. A printed replica of an electronically recorded voiceprint proves each speaker is distinct.
4. Our handwriting is unique. It can be forged, but the person must be an expert.
5. Bloodhounds can pick up the scent of one person out of a million.
6. Brainwave patterns are entirely distinct.
7. Human infants are born with unique and identifiable rhythms of sleeping and waking. A newborn's breathing pattern is as distinct as a thumbprint.
8. Every cell in the body contains molecules of DNA upon which is written the blueprint for the entire body.
9. Even the irises of our eyes are different.

Perhaps it sounds contradictory that Vaisnavas would not see everyone as equal, since Vaisnavas are supposed to be compassionate. Compassion refers to the ability to feel deep sympathy and sorrow for another's suffering or misfortune, accompanied by a desire to alleviate their pain or remove its cause. It is based on the ability to empathize, to "experience" another's pain as if it were our own. Compassion, therefore, is based on a sense of equality. How can Vaisnavas, then, as spiritualists—people who are concerned about all living entities and aware that everything is coming from God—contend that everyone is not equal?

Vaisnavas see "equality" in its most profound sense. Equality to a Vaisnava means that each living entity is an eternal spirit soul, part and parcel of God, and this is the basis of each person's sameness. They understand, however, that all bodies are not equal. There is a hierarchy based on a particular entity's ability to dominate material nature. This refers to natural differences that exist in nature, not arbitrary differences concocted by man.

> *All transformations and variety in respect to living entities are due to the body. As far as spirit is concerned, living entities are the same.*[1]

As spirit souls, we all have equal potential to realize our actual natures and our relationship with the Supreme Lord. However—and this may not be politically correct—we are not equal in desire, interest, material strength or knowledge. The differences between us are caused by how the material modes act upon us according to our desires and past deeds. To see everyone as "the same" on this level is to deny each person's unique abilities and needs.

Therefore, before we can begin to understand the need for monarchy, we must understand the naturalness

---

1   Swami Prabhupada, *Bhagavad-gita*, 13.20 purport

of hierarchy. With that knowledge, we can then examine democracy and appreciate it for what it is, but not be blind toward what it is not.

THE VALUE OF A DIVINELY INSPIRED MONARCH

Monarchy in its most wonderful sense is sacred rule. Vaisnavas appreciate monarchy in its purest sense, for such a system upholds a king who rules on behalf of the Supreme Lord. A king who follows scriptural authority, his spiritual advisors and his divinely inspired predecessor kings will offer knowledge of right and wrong, as well as time-tested techniques of spiritual leadership that work. This cancels the need for speculation about what policies are just, what is good for people, and what is the highest concern.

In the so-called democracy of today, it is said that all people are equal. As we have seen, however, all people are not equal. People are of different grades according to their inherent natures and developed qualities. Thus, an enlightened, God conscious monarch is needed to guide the people toward a higher goal in life, and to represent the people's spiritual needs.

A God conscious monarch or leader will manage from a spiritual paradigm. We often think that having power means having the ability to manipulate. The sign of a civilization that has fallen is its full reliance on external things and its lack of independent power, which, in reality, translates into its lack of spiritual wisdom. The more powerful an individual or civilization, the more they are able to go within, to develop their internal life. When the state degrades, it is a sign that its leadership is focused on external and selfish interests. When a monarch begins to exploit the citizens to achieve his own political ends or the fulfillment of his sectarian interests, then it becomes totalitarianism. Power is wonderful when used properly, but when it is used improperly, it is tremendously dangerous.

Vaisnavas, again, support divine monarchy. Perhaps that sounds radical in light of today's world situation. But we are speaking about sacred rule connected with the ancient tradition of enlightened leadership—monarchs who are spiritually and materially responsive to the needs of the whole kingdom.

The conditioned souls in the material world are trying to play God. When the leaders try to play the same game by gathering as many of the Lord's opulences unto themselves as possible instead of protecting the citizens, we have an unhealthy situation. Humanity becomes transformed into individuals who coerce and manipulate others to gain power. In such a society, people lose their focus on the soul and forget the real nature of the living entity. A divine monarchy is meant to protect them from such an end.

THE IMPORTANCE OF SPEAKER AND HEARER

There have been special times in history when extremely qualified audiences have assembled to hear truth. One was when the *Srimad-Bhagavatam* was spoken, thousands of years ago. Some Vedic scholars feel there has never been an audience as important or powerful as the one that gathered to hear the *Bhagavatam* recited. While the speaker of a message is important, the audience who receives the message is also important. The quality of both helps us to gauge the importance of the exchange. For example, in the U.S. when a significant speaker comes forward, both the Senate and the House of Representatives convene to hear the message: We see by this that something important is happening in the government. When the *Bhagavatam* was spoken both on the bank of the Yamuna and later at Naimisaranya, the message was grave and the personalities who came to hear it were spiritually advanced.

Vedic scholars consider Bhishmadeva's instructions to Yudhisthira on ruling the entire planet another great exchange. This was conveyed in the ancient religious epic, *Mahabharata*, and summarized in the *Bhagavatam*. An interesting difference between these two discourses is that when Sukadeva Gosvami recited the *Bhagavatam*, King Pariksit was preparing to die and had already renounced his kingdom. When Bhishmadeva spoke, however, it was he who was leaving the world and King Yudhisthira who was about to ascend the throne. Bhishmadeva was therefore giving Yudhisthira instructions and encouragement on managerial affairs. King Pariksit was leaving management behind; Yudhisthira was actively entering it. In this book, we will discuss significant issues from both cases.

WHY IS A KING NECESSARY?

A king is necessary because people are sinful. In a perfect society, a king would not be needed, because there would be no need to enforce rules and regulations—people would follow them of their own accord—and therefore no need for protection. As both conditioning and nature cause people to act sinfully, people require the guidance and protection afforded by a pious king. A king's duty is to create a culture that will stimulate people to do the right thing, in the right way, at the right time.

We will discuss Bhishmadeva's instructions from the *Manu-samhita*, an ancient Indian text that provides cutting-edge information about spiritual leadership for the ills of a material society. Thus we will examine what I call "visionary servant-leadership." I would like to discuss these things for several reasons. First, I am always interested in improving my leadership skills. Second, I am interested in evaluating and appreciating just how powerful the position of any given leader is, how much impact leadership can have on people's lives, how urgent it is to have good leaders, and how dangerous it can be when leaders miss the mark. I am also interested in understanding how a monarchical government provides healthy leadership when it is divinely inspired. That is, when it pleases God and provides protection and guidance for people in general.

A LEADER'S FIRST CONQUEST

The *Manu-samhita* mentions how a king or a leader who does not give proper protection to his constituents is a dead king, meaning that a large percentage of leadership lies in providing protection. The *Manu-samhita* goes on to give formulas for how the king and his subjects should relate to one another. For example, the citizens should give to the king's treasury one-fifth of their animals, one-tenth of their precious metals, one-tenth of their grains, a quarter of the merit arising from their pious deeds, and one-sixth of the impious results arising from their sinful deeds. Often we see that when leaders or politicians leave their positions, they quickly fall ill or even die. This is because they are receiving the one-sixth sinful reactions for all the people they have governed, as well as facing the reactions to their own sins. In a country where the government encourages or permits sinful activity to flourish—slaughterhouses, prostitution, lotteries, casinos, legalized intoxication, abortion, etc.—that one-sixth sinful reaction is a force to be reckoned with.

The *Manu-samhita* explains that the greatest conquest a king can make is the conquest of his own senses. Whatever area a leader is weak in is likely the area where he will sell out his people. If someone has a weakness for money, that will be his arena of failure. We see many leaders falling prey to illicit sex. If leaders learn to control their senses and thus gain the strengths needed to overcome their weaknesses, they will not disappoint or embarrass themselves or their citizens. No one can be a strong leader without regulating the senses.

The king makes the age. When leaders are properly in control of their senses, it becomes possible for them to imbibe the inspiration of the divine. That is, divinity will be able to work through them. Ultimately, the divine monarch acts as God's representative in a physical body (*naradeva*), although he always sees himself as merely the servant of God. By protecting the citizens, such a self-controlled, divinely inspired king can protect his people and also distribute a spiritual message in a way that his citizens can both appreciate and follow. If he has not controlled his senses, however, he will manipulate and exploit his citizens rather than offering them true protection. The people will follow his example in various ways, becoming as dishonest and exploitative as their king. Again, the leaders make the people and the people make the leaders.

Great *acaryas*, or spiritual teachers, want to help people out of their confusion. They also want to create or reestablish the *brahmana* class, a priestly class with higher knowledge. They want to teach the proper perspective on philosophical matters, an understanding of body and soul, and create a healthy social order so that people can somehow resolve the conflicts in their lives and societies. Without their guidance, conflicts will accelerate. They expect us all to become leaders in various ways. They expect us all to become spiritual teachers.

BHISHMADEVA'S QUALIFICATIONS

In the *Mahabharata* story, Krishna chose Bhishmadeva to speak about leadership, and Bhismadeva spoke only about monarchy. Let us look at the scene of the battle of Kuruksetra—the devastating war conveyed in the *Mahabharata* epic—before we examine Bhishma's actual words. This is one of the most important wars that humankind has ever faced. By divine arrangement, most of the personalities fighting had come from the celestial abode. They had taken unusual positions in this world in order to bring about serious changes. Literally millions of people were killed during this war, and it caused a total shift of activity on the planet.

The end of the battle saw the Pandavas victorious. This meant that Yudhisthira, leader among the Pandava brothers, became king. The war was ostensibly fought to regain the Pandava throne, which had been usurped by the Kurus, their self-interested cousins. That is, the battle was fought specifically to transfer the kingship from Duryodhana to Yudhisthira. Duryodhana, while atheistic, was basically *dharmic* in the way he ruled. The people were not significantly suffering during his reign, and the kingdom appeared to be running smoothly. In Yudhisthira's mind, Duryodhana could have continued to rule and the citizens would have been happy. But this was not to be, and war ensued.

Yudhisthira was forced into battle and witnessed the number of deaths this conflict had caused. In his grief, all he could see was the many deaths that came from this venture to regain his throne. He could not bear the thought of becoming king at the cost of so many lives. Many counselors and advisors tried to speak to Yudhisthira, to convince him of both his innocence and his duty, but to no avail. Even Krishna tried to comfort him, but without success. Then Krishna decided to ask Grandfather Bhishmadeva to speak to him. Bhishmadeva was the dear grandfather of both the Kauravas and the Pandavas, and Krishna empowered him to help Yudhisthira overcome his grief. Bhishmadeva was an unusually great personality, and he had been given the power to decide when he would die and leave his body. No one could actually kill him. In fact, he was shot during the battle, and was lying on a bed of arrows that pierced his body. He thus met his final days on the battlefield, surrounded by sages. He gave his enlightened discourse while in this condition.

The highest philosophy is often presented under the most difficult circumstances. The *Bhagavad-gita* was spoken on a battlefield while Krishna and Arjuna stood between two armies prepared for battle. The *Mahabharata* is also set in the context of the circumstances leading up to this great war. When Krishna and Yudhisthira approached Bhishmadeva, his body was devastated, and he was preparing to depart this world. The message he delivered at that time was profound. When one is in such a serious predicament, there is little inclination to speak whimsically. Words of wisdom are often spoken as someone is leaving his or her body; impending death can focus the consciousness on the essential.

Bhishmadeva is known particularly as a supporter of *dharma*, a Sanskrit word that refers to duty, nature, religion, truth, righteousness, and integrity. *Dharma* is such a powerful word that there is no English equivalent, no word that can encompass its full meaning. Krishna identified Bhishma as among the most righteous people on the planet. This being so, Bhishma definitely had the right to speak about *dharma*. It is natural to be concerned about a speaker's qualifications; according to God Himself, Bhishma was a fully qualified speaker.

A COMPLEX SCIENCE

> *"Some of the most intricate knots of the mysteries of the universe are wrapped up in leadership. It is not easy to rule well, and a king's one worldly duty is to rule well. He is essentially a man of action."* [2]

In modern times, we can see just how difficult leadership is. In the secular world, leadership is becoming a joke. People tend to make fun of their leaders. Cartoons and caricatures of them are not uncommon, and talk show hosts make fun of them on a regular basis. People write sarcastic books about them, and the media is constantly watching for opportunities to make them look ridiculous. This is augmented by the fact that many leaders are under legal investigation for questionable activities. This is true not only in the United States but in countries around the world. When we examine leadership in all arenas—spiritual, academic, etc.—we see that there are perhaps more cheaters than people who are actually qualified.

Leaders have an impact on the general populace. When people do not trust their leaders, their relationships with one

---

[2] This quote and all of the following highlighted quotes that appear in Part 1 are the instructions of Bhishmadeva.

another are affected as well. When people are afraid of their authorities, their fear spreads into other areas of their lives and gradually develops into paranoia and mistrust in their interactions with others. Trust and faith do not arise out of thin air. They are evoked by an environment that nurtures those feelings.

In ancient times, people trusted their kings because they were clear about the king's duties and activities. People understood the consequences for illegal or improper actions, and they trusted the king to help them in times of need. Such clarity allowed people to be at ease while performing their duties, and to be inspired in their own dutiful occupations by the trust that the king himself was dutiful and honest. Tremendous problems result when there is no proper leadership—like a family without parents, where the children are left without protection or guidance.

Ironically, the people who would make the best leaders often avoid positions of leadership. This is true both in secular and spiritual environments. Those who are eager for positions often possess the least qualifications. Instead of desiring to serve others, they have a desire to control them. Leadership provides them with a field to use power for control. When citizens do not have sufficiently developed consciousness to stimulate good leadership, and when leadership has become so degraded that it has influenced people toward greater degradation, the world's manipulators, cheaters, and otherwise motivated personalities will take control. We can see this by examining almost any country in the world, either in terms of its history or in terms of its current situation.

Many American presidents have become millionaires because their power came with money, prestige and political alliance. Tyrants align with other tyrants, exploiters with other exploiters. Those who could best serve humanity cannot always enter the leadership arena; in today's world, it is often impossible to become a leader without taking advantage of an underworld element. It sometimes seems that this is a world of cheaters and the cheated, where the main interests are selfishness and the propagation of sinful culture.

Bhishma says a king is essentially a man of action, not of destiny. Action has a significant effect on destiny. There are now people in leadership who at one extreme, are afraid to lead or at the other extreme, manipulate the people, abusing their roles as leaders. They control people without actually leading them in a positive direction. If leaders are afraid to lead, then they are not actually leading. To lead others means to understand the field of activities and what is necessary for the welfare of others. Understanding these things, a genuine leader must guide, coordinate and act based on what he knows to be true. To lead means to guide from the front—by one's own example.

Bhishmadeva states that leaders must be prepared to act. Leaders try to control destiny rather than allowing destiny to control them. Leaders do not wait for things to happen; rather, they make them happen. Leaders are not fully subjected to their environment nor the present circumstances under which they find themselves; leaders create the environment.

THE KING'S DUTY IS SPIRITUAL

> "A king's highest duty is to the gods. Next, and of equal importance, is his duty to truth. Truth is the highest refuge. All the world rests on truth."

A king must consistently remind himself that he is ultimately answerable to God. Therefore, he should not be distracted by the idea that he can please each of his citizens, which, of course, is impractical. Being a leader is not about winning a popularity contest. Sometimes leaders are coerced into giving favors or supporting particular interests due to sentimentality or a false sense of indebtedness, but if leaders consider themselves accountable to God, they will not be easily influenced away from principles of morality.

Bhishmadeva explains elsewhere that a king's highest duty is to Krishna, the Absolute Truth. God and truth go hand-in-hand. When the relative truths of the material world are favorable to our service to Krishna, we can align ourselves with them, but we should understand that these relative principles and truths are always subordinate to the Supreme Lord.

Material truths are always relative, and this often causes ambiguity. For example, Bhishmadeva says that kings should know how to conceal their plans, that they should know how to be diplomatic. At the same time, he states that the king must place great emphasis on the pursuit of truth. Although these two statements appear contradictory, we should understand that Bhishmadeva is instructing Yudhisthira on how to manage the material world with the intention of bringing about the highest good. This is analogous to managing a prison. The material world is essentially a prison for conditioned souls. It is filled with living entities with criminal mentalities, who use and abuse what God has provided without giving Him credit or accepting that they are accountable to Him. The king's main concern is to rehabilitate the prisoners. Managing the material energy is really about helping criminals become free. Rehabilitation can be enacted by a variety of methods.

If everyone were already free, of course, management would be different. Bhishmadeva was not speaking of a pure devotee managing other pure devotees, but of how a divinely inspired king could deal with people suffering from varying degrees of sinful mentality.

Our own application of management principles centers around the great spiritualist and scholar of religion, Rupa Gosvami, who said *nirbandha-krsna-sambhandhe, yukta-vairagyam ucyate*:

> When one is not attached to anything but at the same time accepts everything in relation to Krishna [God], one is rightly situated above possessiveness. On the other hand, one who rejects everything without knowledge of its relationship to Krishna is not as complete in his renunciation.[3]

---

3   Rupa Goswami, *Bhakti-Rasamrta Sindhu*, 1.2.255

This means that in applying leadership principles—or in choosing which principles to follow in our own lives—we should accept those that are favorable to our service to God and reject all those that are unfavorable. This is the basis of discrimination.

But how can we discriminate between favorable and unfavorable? We see that great spiritual teachers throughout history always support tradition while at the same time bringing about needed changes, or adaptations, in the details of how a spiritual culture is followed. These changes are made according to time, place, and the persons involved. While this may work when employed by spiritually evolved beings, how can the average person know when he or she is adapting in an inappropriate way or according to conditioning? In other words, how can we know how to not disturb the essence while changing details according to time and place? When one of my mentors, A.C. Bhaktivedanta Swami Srila Prabhupada, was asked this question, he said, "It is not an easy thing to know." It takes a certain amount of spiritual advancement to know what can be changed and what cannot. It becomes important to understand what constitutes elevated consciousness, and thus what constitutes a proper leader. If we learn to recognize true visionary leadership, we can trust in the changes that are being made.

Srila Prabhupada made many changes for the modern day Vaisnava community. For example, he reduced the number of rounds from 64 to 16, that is, the number of times one chants a full round of prayers on one's rosary beads. He gave brahminical initiation to women—a departure from Indian tradition. He gave *sannyasa* (the prestigious renounced order of life) to young Western men, whereas, traditionally, one had to be in the last stages of one's life. Many of these adjustments were made out of his desire to serve his *guru's* instruction to preach God consciousness in the Western countries. He was compassionate enough to see what was needed by these Westerners, who did not share the same cultural experiences as the Indian monks.

Similarly, Ramanujacarya, a great teacher from medieval India, made changes by codifying Deity worship, and Madhvacarya, another prominent Vaisnava leader, made changes in the lineage's emphasis on dualism. But not just any saintly person can make such fundamental changes with the same positive effect. Again, it is important to know how to evaluate leadership. Otherwise, we may wonder whether the concessions being made for time and place are merely a reflection of a leader's inability to follow a path that might be more stringent.

Bhishmadeva's instructions help us to understand that powerful leaders do powerful things, make powerful changes, lead in powerful ways, and have a powerful vision with penetrating focus. Their intense power, in fact, always creates an atmosphere of danger. Because of this, some say democracy may be a safer choice, as if there is more safety in many people coming together to make a mistake than one or a few leaders making a mistake on everyone's behalf. It should be noted, however, that in a proper Vedic system, the king does not make his decisions unilaterally. A Vedic king is not a dictator. Rather, he is a leader who takes counsel from *brahmanas*, saintly priests, and the precedents set by earlier divinely inspired monarchs. Again, the spiritual leader's first commitment is to God. We should keep this in mind as we move on to other points.

A TRUE LEADER IS ABOVE DUPLICITY

> *"The king should be straightforward in both words and conduct."*

Modern leadership often means, "Do as I say, not as I do." The leader leads both a public life and a private life, and these two are usually quite different. The leader should be an *acarya*, one who leads by example.

> *"He should know when to conceal his own weakness (the weakness in His kingdom)."*

Again, there is an apparent contradiction. First, Bhishma says that a leader should be straightforward in his action and speech, and now he says he should know when to conceal his own weaknesses. How do we understand this contradiction? His enemies will take advantage of weaknesses in his kingdom and try to destabilize or sabotage his rule. Therefore, any weaknesses in one's administration will be great targets for the competition. A leader should give close attention to making strategic improvements whenever there are such weaknesses.

Sometimes, in order to help others, a true leader must not always reveal his intent. While he must be honest and straightforward in all his dealings, he can simultaneously hold back information that might be detrimental to the spiritual goals of his people. He must also be diplomatic in dealing with his adversaries.

THE OPULENCE OF POWER

In the *Srimad-Bhagavatam* we find that God has six opulences—renunciation, wealth, beauty, fame, strength, and knowledge—and each of these provides Him with alternative ways to express His power. In one sense, social evolution is about the search for and alignment with power. People search for power both individually and collectively, and it is this search that creates societies. We have already discussed how the king is not controlled by destiny but rather controls destiny. Similarly, the king is not controlled by the particular age in which he appears. Rather, he sets the tone for the age by his standards of consciousness and rule. How the leader uses power determines how the people under his charge evolve. Conversely, the state of evolution in a society determines the type of power the individuals in that society will be inclined to access. Darwin was not far off when he said that life is about the struggle for power, or survival of the fittest.

In primitive societies, physical power rules. This is also true among animals. The leader is the one with the most physical strength and a willingness to use it in a particular way. As an example, I cite the bulls we now have at one of our projects in Ghana. Other farmers in the area also have bulls. Sometimes while grazing, the bulls fight one another. Interestingly, their senseless battling comes to a halt when they realize that one is stronger than the other. The winning bull then claims the cows as his prize, while the defeated bulls wander off. The next time the defeated bull comes near the winner, it does not fight but continues to recognize the winner's superior strength.

In more developed societies, social power has more effect than physical strength. Social power is resource power, relationship power, institutional power. It is based on who one knows and what one knows. Most of today's societies are based on social power. With whom one is connected determines how well one is able to function. For example, proximity to the Presidency determines how much power one can wield.

Another type of power is emotional power. This also influences many people. Various entertainers wield emotional power. People worship actors, singers, athletes, etc. These entertainers are able to manipulate an audience's feelings. In return, they achieve new heights of fame and wealth. They are respected, sought after and emulated.

Then there is mental power, which wields most of its effectiveness through the academic world. Academia is a culture of its own, but it still makes a tremendous impact on the way we think and what kinds of things we think about. What modern-day professors represent as knowledge and truth, we come to believe as actually being so. As society continues to evolve, mental power becomes more important and scholarship more respected. The fact that this is no longer true in this country is a sign of our social degradation. Many of the scholars, scientists, and *brahmanas* in Kali-yuga are frustrated; they have no way to share their knowledge. Many of our best scientists are working on classified projects, and are forced to either lie about what they are doing or are not able to reveal their work. This mental power has also been used to exploit people, as we have seen in the development of nuclear and biological weapons and other destructive technologies. At the same time, it has been used to benefit others—to discover cures for diseases, to create vaccinations for epidemics and for other such purposes. Thus, mental and intellectual power is a distinct category.

There is also intuitive power. Often, artists or other people in touch with creative energy and those involved in the paranormal, possess this kind of power. People working with intuitive powers are important in more evolved societies, where they serve as seers or workers with the subtle arts. All of these forms of power are subservient to sacred power, which, when properly accessed, can incorporate all of the prior forms.

SACRED POWER, DIVINE POWER

Our focus here is sacred power, which comes from within. It is based on selfless, attentive service to God and spiritual law. Of course, there are different levels of sacred power. In a social sense, it is rooted in *varnasrama-dharma*, or the division of society according to natural and spiritual laws. But beyond *varnasrama*, and therefore beyond monarchy, there is the divine power of being totally in line with Krishna's will.

Let us examine the relative positions of *ksatriyas* (kings) and *brahmanas* (priests). A *ksatriya* has a different position than a *brahmana*. Bhishmadeva's instructions on chivalry and the art of management are given to a *ksatriya*, and these instructions may not always be in accord with the instructions given to *brahmanas*, who are asked to practice straightforward honesty. *Ksatriya* life always requires diplomacy, but a spiritually-minded *ksatriya* will only use diplomacy to bring about a higher good. For that higher good, he is ready to meet challenge, conflict and war. One who is taking up the service of a *ksatriya* must be able to be both mild and, when necessary, fierce. *Brahmanas* are not prone to diplomacy. They speak the truth, whether it is palatable or not.

A sacred leader working under sacred power always thinks about the people's welfare. A proper leader, as Bhishma explains, should know his constituents as well as a mother knows her children, and he should protect and care for them with great enthusiasm. A mother may sometimes reprimand her children, and other times she submits to their appeals. The two extremes of a *ksatriya's* mood—his ability to be both mild and fierce—are reconciled when he adopts the mood of a mother. His ultimate concern is to care for and protect his citizens, and he is prepared to do whatever is necessary to attain that goal. Because we don't see, in modern leadership, a strong desire to protect others, even in spiritual circles, problems are inevitable. Every social problem is connected either to the lack of proper leadership or to the inability to recognize and trust proper leadership when it is present. Bhishma confirms this point by declaring that the king makes the age; the leader's consciousness determines the quality of the age—its atmosphere and the mood of the people.

Now let us again turn to Bhishma's instructions to Yudhisthira. A Vaisnava is interested in seeing others' needs met, especially their greatest spiritual needs. Therefore, those who are most enlightened have the best potential and the requisite ability to lead. Such persons should be given management positions, so that society can be uplifted. Consensus (democracy) may sound good, but when the majority is foolish, ignorant, or simply uninformed, their decisions cannot be trusted or relied upon. When judgment is not sound, unwise leaders are invariably chosen. Those leaders will then maintain their citizens at the same low standard. Again, it takes good leadership and recognition of good leadership to create a wholesome society.

GOOD LEADERSHIP IS BALANCED

> "There is a danger in mildness. The king should not be too mild, or he will be disregarded. The people will not have enough respect for him and his words. He must also avoid the other extreme (of being too fierce), for then the people will fear him, which does not create a happy state of affairs."

If leaders are too mild, people will disregard them. They will not take such leaders seriously and will not therefore be deterred from acting according to their lower natures. In the material world, the tendency to cheat is strong; people also make mistakes and suffer from other weaknesses. Leaders may wish to be mild out of sentiment, but in a world where people are willing to cheat, such mildness will be exploited.

Neither should leaders be too fierce. When fear is the motivating factor, people will do what is necessary to save their careers and lives but will not imbibe the principles on a deeper level. Like children who are heavily disciplined, such people will be righteous in public, but as soon as they are alone, they will do what they want. Force and repression are not effective ways to teach others a higher mode of behavior; they do not require people to have any understanding of the reasons behind the law.

Thus, both extreme mildness and extreme fierceness are dangerous. Leaders should be neither too tolerant nor too intolerant.

A current question in the United States that addresses the issue of mildness vs. fierceness is the question of capital punishment. Should the government have the right to kill criminals or not? A spiritual leader understands the laws of *karma*. A Vaisnava, in this case, would again appear conservative. They support capital punishment because they understand that when a person commits sin, he will eventually have to pay karmic consequences, which refers to the fact that every action has a reaction. Even if a person feels compunction, recognizing his wrong, he still has a karmic debt to pay. Capital punishment allows this debt to be paid immediately, so the soul can go on without obstruction.

However, in present day society capital punishment should probably be abolished. This is so because there is a fairly high percentage of people who are imprisoned wrongly, based on deals criminals make with the state, or mistaken identity, or faulty witnesses, and sometimes due to corruption. The *Manu-samhita* states that in the case of a wrong judgment, the king must bear one-fourth of the *karma* for having killed the wrong man. The rest of the blame is split equally among the false witnesses, the mistaken advisors (*brahmanas* guiding the king in criminal justice), and on the person who actually committed the crime. In the case of a just decision, the reaction for the crime falls solely on the perpetrator, and the king is not held responsible for condemning him to death.

In the *Srimad-Bhagavatam* there is a story of Indra and Brihaspati that illustrates this point. Indra was once sitting on his throne, being worshiped elaborately by his followers, when Brihaspati entered the assembly. Brihaspati is Indra's spiritual master, but due to pride, Indra ignored Brihaspati and failed to offer him respect. Brihaspati realized Indra's mental condition and immediately left the room. Indra understood that he had offended Brihaspati. Although Indra realized his mistake and even apologized to his *guru*, he had committed an offense and was due a karmic reaction. He paid by losing his kingdom to the demons.

We should understand Bhishma's points and their ramifications because in our own communities and lives, they help us understand why certain things happen. They can also help us to better understand how to deal with problems and how to improve ourselves when we are acting improperly. They can help us face the fact that everything we do brings a consequence. Otherwise, we will be bewildered.

We are sometimes bewildered by the things that happen to us, but we should understand that everything we are experiencing is a direct result of something we have done in the past—either in this lifetime or in a previous lifetime. We are not always aware of the gravity of our offenses, so we do not feel enough remorse for them. Therefore, we suffer reactions that are meant to bring us to our senses and to a deeper understanding. Similarly, we are rarely aware of the extent of blessings we have received from our pious activities.

If we understand even a little about karmic law, we will always treat others with compassion and love and offer them sincere service. Vaisnavas try to never give offense but to always remain humble. When one is truly humble, he cannot be offensive.

Humility is the quality of a spiritualist. All good leadership is spiritual, even though materialists may not realize that. This is because good leaders try to bring out the best in people. It doesn't matter what the organization or coalition, bringing out the best in others means celebrating their spiritual nature. Spiritual leaders address the ultimate point of human life—progress on the spiritual path, and teach their followers to reinstate themselves in devotional service to God. It is a difficult job because people are more interested in usurping God's position than in serving Him. Their usual desire is not spiritual but rather to obtain as much wealth, fame or power for themselves as they can in order to fully enjoy their senses.

As we try to understand the difference between material and spiritual leadership, and to practice spiritual leadership, we will be able to create a global mind shift. Such leaders can also help all people on this planet to remember what they have forgotten—the ultimate goal of life, self-realization. True leaders guide people by their personal examples, they show people what is possible, and help make that which seems impossible—a spiritual world on earth—a reality. Material consciousness is almost impossible to transcend, but through divine leadership, material entanglements can be minimized and spiritual pursuits maximized.

But without power, no one can accomplish anything. Most of the world's greatest criminals, greatest deviants, have used power to make alliances. Much of the material scheme is nothing more than highly sinful people aligning themselves against sincere, spiritual people, the sinful trying to captivate and sway the minds of the innocent, while the godly persons try to stimulate their minds toward spiritual culture. Everything is based on power.

Spiritual leaders have their own weapons with which they regain power from the godless. For example, they chant *mantras* and perform *yajnas*, sacrifices, as a way to clear the atmosphere and their minds of the pollution from materialistic sound vibration and activities. When the atmosphere is polluted, people tend to take shelter of deviant power structures and become comfortable with sinful activity. When spiritual leaders rise to the fore, however, it is like cutting through materialism and clearly demarcating the good from the bad. People are then better equipped to make a proper choice.

There is presently a crisis in world leadership. People and leaders alike are unclear about spiritual law. There have not been sufficient examples of spirituality in practice to help others follow a correct path; rather, incredible deviation from spirituality has been tolerated throughout the centuries.

I have a college friend who has become a judge. He told me recently, "You know, I feel horrible. I have arranged for so many cheaters to go free. Embezzlers, murderers—I knew they were lying as well as they did. Many of them are out in society cheating people again. Because I was a good lawyer, I got them off." He said, "I have all this on my conscience—my success in rising to the position of judge is based on my having been a good cheater."

He added that such cheating often happens in the legal system because people do not demand much of their leaders. They compromise, he said, because they themselves are so materialistic. Consequently, the leaders are materialistic and they deal with materialistic people. Their ability to hold power is based on how well they can facilitate degradation. My friend was remorseful because, as we talked, he could see that I was still concerned about humanity, spirituality and had remained principle-centered. Although my friend had become wealthy, he was not principle-centered and certainly hadn't understood sacred leadership. Therefore, he was miserable.

A LEADER MUST BE COMPASSIONATE BUT STRONG

> *"Compassion must be a part of the leader's mental make-up, but he must guard against displaying a too-forgiving nature, because then he will be considered weak by low men, and they will take advantage of him."*

Again, a leader should not be too mild. Neither should he appear too forgiving if he wants to see actual rectification in his subjects. If one of his subjects commits an offense, that person must be punished to bring about the necessary rectification and to dismiss the karmic reaction.

Also, if a leader is too forgiving, "low men" will try to take advantage of his kindness and will continue their sinful activities without fear.

A leader who is too sentimental is actually a disservice to the people. If we examine political history, we will see that most revolutions and *coups d'etat* are carried out by those closest to the leader. The further away one is from the seat of power, the more difficult it is to gain it. When leaders do not know the art of leadership, they will fall prey to those whom they have given favors, and to those whose corruption they have supported. Of course, corruption breeds more corruption. Thus, violence born of corruption breeds more violence and more corruption in a seemingly endless cycle.

One reason many third-world countries break out in violence during an election is because people understand that whoever becomes the country's leader will become instantly wealthy and powerful. Often third-world leaders become millionaires overnight, because many of the country's assets belong to the leader. When I spoke to my friend former President Nelson Mandela for the first time, I asked him if he knew why Blacks and Indians didn't vote for him *en masse*, despite their opposition to the apartheid system. I explained how most people are sensitive to what Black leadership in general has meant to Black Africa. I was referring to a recent conference in Togo, where one of the issues discussed was embezzlement. It was revealed that African Heads of State had remitted about twenty-two billion dollars to their foreign bank accounts in less than one year. This indicated, of course, that the leaders had taken much of the countries' assets for themselves. I told Mr. Mandela that it was up to him to send out the message that leadership does not have to mean that the leader lines his pocket while the people continue to suffer.

Previous President Mbutu of Zaire was one of the richest men in the world, but Zaire is one of the poorest countries. It doesn't take a detailed understanding of economics to know what is going on. Mbutu had filtered much of the country's resources out for himself. Zaire has many important minerals essential for nuclear development. The American government is interested in nuclear development, and in the past has supported dictators, tyrants, and embezzlers. Cheating leaders around the world maintain one another. Cheaters by definition look for ways to enhance their own positions; their main interest is personal sense gratification. Little do they realize that they will have to pay a heavy consequence for their corruption. In country after country, we see leaders interested in economic development at the expense of the human condition. All this is due to both poor leadership and people's ignorance of how to impose higher standards on their leaders.

A LEADER MUST KNOW FRIEND AND FOE ALIKE

> *"A king should be alert. He must study his foes and friends incessantly."*

A good leader knows his enemies as well as his allies. A good leader studies his allies because he is not independent in his strength. Military training requires that soldiers develop strong teamwork skills; in battle, each individual soldier is both accountable for the lives of his colleagues and dependent upon them for his own survival. Therefore, Bhishmadeva advises a king to study his friends as well as his enemies. His life may depend upon it.

Military leaders also understand the importance of not only stocking their own arsenals but knowing what weapons the enemy has. It would be crazy to fight an enemy with sticks and stones if they are using guns. Therefore, Bhishma makes it clear that it is important to study the competition.

Bhishma's points are important in the spiritual realm as well. Much of life in this world is based on relativities. The *Bhagavad-gita*, *Bible*, *Koran* and other scriptures delineate the differences between the divine and demonic natures. By understanding both, we can find the purely spiritual path.

CONSIDERING ONE'S PEOPLE BEFORE ONESELF

> *"A king's duty is to his people. He should take care of them with no thoughts of pleasing himself. He should subordinate his own wishes and desires to those of the people."*

A leader's first duty is to his people. Then only should he seek his own comforts, appetites, aspirations, and pleasures. Good leadership means thinking first of the welfare of others before thinking of oneself.

PARENTAL SPIRIT

> *"He should guard them as a mother guards a child.... A leader should know his or her constituents as much or better than a mother knows her children."*

An effective leader should know his dependents as well as a mother knows her child, and he should care for them in the same parental spirit. This is the highest standard of leadership, and is most pleasing to God Himself.

The principle of protection is significant. The *Manu-samhita* states, "A king who does not protect his citizens is a dead king." Protection is a serious rule of law.

INDEPENDENCE

> *"The king needs to be careful not to place implicit confidence in anyone. He should keep his innermost thoughts concealed from even his nearest and dearest."*

Today's friend may be tomorrow's enemy or spy. Best to be cautious. We see this principle in parts of Nigeria, where the traditional system of monarchy is still in effect. I am a high chief in Nigeria, and I use that position to preach higher consciousness to politicians, CEOs, kings and chiefs. In some cases, these traditional leaders have ancient ancestral lineages that extend back for many generations. Such kings do not eat in public, and they will only eat if the food has been cooked by a specific cook—and only after the cook has tasted the food first to see if it has been poisoned.

THE FEAR OF THE FACELESS

> *"A king should fear his kinsmen as he would fear death, but he shouldn't reveal his fear to them."*

In Nigeria and in other countries as well, the successor to the throne is not allowed to even live in the same province as the king. This is because he may try to kill the king to take his post.

Bhishmadeva's instructions are taken from India's ancient monarchical wisdom. As we go deeper into any ancient culture, we will find that those cultures are close to Vedic culture. The Vedic civilization was once spread throughout the world, and aside from kingly wisdom, it provided people with an opportunity to learn how to come closer to God. The remnants of Vedic culture remain centered in India, but anyone can tap into its reservoir of knowledge for the betterment of mankind.

RECOGNIZING ONE'S OWN WEAKNESS

> *"A king needs to know when to seek protection in his fort. When his position is weak, he should be ready to make peace with a foe who is stronger."*

A king must also be able to recognize his own weakness. Sometimes leaders become so attached to power that they fail to discharge their duties properly and thus do not protect the people. Or, instead of resigning after they become ineffective, they will do everything to remain in their positions. Such a leader may even realize the impropriety of his actions, but be so overwhelmed by his desire for profit, adoration and distinction that he cannot control himself. A leader must learn to identify nescience while cultivating transcendence. If he is sincere, he will rise beyond his lesser nature and become the leader he was meant to be.

CONTROLLING ONE'S DESIRES

> *"Covetousness is the root of all sins. It destroys all merit and goodness."*

Bhishma spoke of self-restraint as a king's highest duty. Now he explains that covetousness (lust) is dangerous. History reveals how powerful leaders have lost huge kingdoms and committed many atrocities due to greed. *Maya*, illusion personified, attacks us at our weakest points. We should always remind ourselves that whenever we fail to maintain our integrity and sense control, that is when we will be unable to feel concern for others. Lust can cause us to betray our own families, what to speak of our constituents or organizations. A true leader must endeavor with full conviction to overcome lust in all its forms.

TRUTH AND WEALTH

> *"Truth is the greatest penance, the highest yoga, and the greatest tirtha or holy place in which to bathe. The wealth of all persons except the brahmanas belongs to the king."*

One-fifth of one's farm animals, one-tenth of one's grains, one-fourth of one's merits, one-sixth of one's sins and one-sixth of one's income should be given to the king's treasury. Here Bhishma adds that the wealth of all persons in the kingdom, except that of the *brahmanas*, belongs to the king.

Why is the *brahmanas'* wealth in a separate category? Qualified *brahmanas* are detached, so cannot be bribed or controlled. A *brahmana's* advice is given freely, and is not dependent upon what he will receive in return. In Vedic culture, the *brahmana* always monitored the *ksatriya*, or the kingly warrior; the *ksatriya* does not rule the *brahmana*. All social and spiritual orders of life are intended to complement one another to make society peaceful.

THE WISDOM OF AGE

> *"The king's ministers should be age fifty or over. Knowledge helps one to be free of desires."*

In this instruction, the value of wisdom and experience is emphasized. We influence others through our actions or consciousness. We even influence the many entities living inside our bodies. These entities are karmically connected to us. In that sense, each living entity leads other living entities. Even the tiniest germs can have a heavy impact upon the body and consciousness of much larger living beings. Therefore, we are all involved in establishing conditions under which those who share our life space will experience the world. Again, as Bhishmadeva explains, the leader's consciousness determines the rate of evolution.

HARBOR NO MALICE

> *"Harbor no malice."*

A leader must not harbor malice toward others. Sometimes people find themselves in a leadership position and simply complain about others. They fail to realize that solving problems is part of what it means to be a leader. That leaders are often not given credit and are the first to be blamed when something goes wrong is also part of what it means to be a leader. A leader who expects to receive credit for what he has accomplished is not really a good leader. A leader who becomes too disturbed by the problems in his or her kingdom is also not a good leader. Problems must not only be tolerated, but also managed. If someone is not willing to do that work, he or she should not accept a leadership position.

Because leaders represent authority, it is not unusual that they receive the brunt of society's insults, anger, or frustration. We are here in the material world because we don't want authority. We are running away from the Supreme Autocrat, better known as God. Whoever represents the Supreme

Autocrat in this world (i.e., a leader) should expect as much hate as love. People tend to rebel against authority figures.

Still, good leaders will remain sensitive to the innocent people's needs and continue to trust their basic intentions. It is the nature of the conditioned soul to have imperfections and to make mistakes. Our sense desires lead us to be biased in various ways, and we cannot easily see the truth. Good leaders will recognize both their own and others' follies, and, in a parental mood, try to care for their subjects. Parents love their children, but they are also aware of their children's limitations. They know when and where to place their trust in their children. If parents are too trusting, they may fail to effectively guide their dependents.

THE IMPORTANCE OF ALLIANCES

> *"Nothing, not even the smallest act, can be accomplished by a single man. He has to have assistance."*

No matter how competent a king may be, he does not have the power to do everything himself. We see in many societies that when leaders try to do all the work single-handedly, they often end up feeling burdened and resentful. Either they become depressed and want to change their service, or they become condescending toward others. The person who tries to do everything himself minimizes the fact that God is the real doer. Such persons are likely to see themselves as the ultimate controller and proprietor. If we make ourselves available, the Lord can work through us.

Bhishma's statement emphasizes the need for leaders to delegate. Our energies should be concentrated. There are many people in this world who could do magnificent things, but because they are trying to do all the work themselves, they become frustrated in their efficiency.

Learning to delegate tasks is an art. First, we must be sure that the task is clearly defined. Otherwise, it is almost certain that we will become disturbed when the work is not done according to our expectations. Second, we should understand that accountability cannot be delegated. For example, I may give to one of my secretaries so many duties that he becomes bewildered in trying to do them all. But I have explained to him that he is responsible to see that all the tasks get done; he does not necessarily have to do everything himself. One cannot delegate accountability, because someone must be responsible for the work getting done. When we delegate work, we should still consider it our task. At least, we should monitor whether the work is getting done. One way to do that is to receive regular reports from the person(s) actually doing the work. Then, if necessary, we can make adjustments to ensure that the assignments are completed. Effective delegation includes providing the delegates with the authority and resources to get the job done.

Delegation is important not only because it relieves the leaders of their burdens but also because an organization thrives when all of its members feel they have a defined and important role to play in it. If leaders make plans without the help of the participants, he will not get the maximum results—even if the leaders' ideas are good. When people feel they are an important part of a project's development, they will be more willing to make sacrifices on the project's behalf. Delegation allows leaders to encourage such participation.

Delegation can be done according to linear principles or from a matrix. In linear management, leaders delegate tasks through a hierarchy. One person will give an instruction to someone under him, who will then give an instruction to someone under him, and each person in line is responsible to the person directly above him. Matrix management is different. One person will delegate tasks to others based on their qualifications to get the job done.

When delegating tasks, it is important to ensure that the person taking on the work has the ability and propensity to do it successfully. People have different propensities and talents. When we can give someone a task in accordance with their natural abilities, they are more likely to accomplish it properly. People who are naturally engaged according to their propensities tend to have a greater sense of well-being.

Most people are dissatisfied with their work. They work more out of duty, or out of a desire for money, than out of heartfelt commitment. The American government initiated a study many years ago to find out why the Japanese excelled in practically all areas of management and production, even though the United

States had more institutions for the development of business. They discovered that facility, knowledge, etc., are responsible for only 15 to 20 percent of management success. What had the most effect was the way a manager interacted with his employees. Managers who include and enthuse their employees are able to build better team spirit and thus be more effective in their projects. Japanese culture reinforces qualities such as integrity, commitment, team spirit, and selflessness. In martial arts, this is called the Bushido principle, which literally means "valuing honor above life." It includes making vows, self-dedication, and denying one's personal interests to serve the whole.

If leaders do not utilize their manpower properly, their employees feel underused or neglected. This causes isolation and resentment. People who feel they have nothing to offer feel unappreciated, and this affects the synergy of the team.

When some members of the team are resentful, apathy develops. A good leader empowers people and does not leave them unmotivated. When people are apathetic, they begin to expect the leader to carry out all the project's plans; they don't feel needed and they don't perform. This in turn puts more pressure on the leader.

If people are resentful enough, they may even try to sabotage the leader's efforts. They become eager to see the leader fail.

Despite the value inherent in making employees team members, why do some leaders refuse to delegate responsibility? Often, it is because they are too attached to profit and distinction. They are afraid to share the credit for the project's success. Other times they may think that no one can do the job as they think it should be done—as well as they themselves can do it. But it is rare to find people who are competent in every area. Those who think they are such rare souls are usually mistaken. Part of good management means knowing to whom one can turn to get particular tasks performed with quality. If we are clear about our own weaknesses, we can then get help where we need it.

To face our weaknesses means being willing to look at ourselves, and before we can expect others to be willing to sacrifice, we should be willing to sacrifice ourselves. Mahatma Gandhi said, "You must be the change you want to see in the world." When we want others to acknowledge our sacrifice, we have not made it selflessly. Sacrifice implies selflessness. When leaders feel parental toward their constituents, then sacrifice comes naturally. When parents announce to their children, "I made this sacrifice for you," it sounds strange. Sacrifice and service are natural in a parent-child relationship, and the parent should not have to shove his or her sacrifices down a child's throat.

Delegation, as mentioned, does not only mean passing-on tasks that need to be done; it also means providing the necessary authority and resources to accomplish the task successfully. Giving authority and resources to others is synonymous with sharing power. We often see powerful leaders surrounded by powerful people. Either these people have been empowered by the leader to act to their capacity, or the leader has connected with equally powerful people in order to accomplish more.

To sum up, those who are successful do not do all the work themselves—they do not even always know all the details of what has to be accomplished. Rather, they are aware of the essentials. They are also conscious of quality. We can never do everything, read everything, or know everything. That is why the *Manu-samhita* recommends that the monarch employ ministers and spies to specialize in needed areas while remaining accountable to him. In this way, he is able to feel the pulse of the populace with an even greater awareness than if he had to learn everything on his own.

Empowering others is based on understanding that they are already powerful but that they may not be aware of their own strengths. A leader who wishes to empower others will arrange situations where others can find their power. A leader cannot empower those whom he considers imbeciles. Neither is empowerment based on forcing others to do things they do not want to do. Rather, it is based on appreciation for who they already are and for the potential within them.

In the spiritual context, we are also aware that God has no favorites. If there is something God wants done, as devotees, we want to share the blessings available through that work with as many people as possible.

If we delegate work simply because we do not want to do it or because we feel it is below us, the people who take it on themselves will not feel empowered. Rather, they will feel dumped upon. They may do the work anyway, but not with the same sense of commitment as if it had been a genuine sharing of responsibility. Such dumping does not yield the results attained when leaders and their helpers work as teams.

AN IMPRESSIVE IMPRESSION

> *"A king who is honored by his subjects will naturally be respected by his foes, and will be feared by them also."*

This is an important point. In many countries, I visit the king. If he gives me his blessings, he sends word out to his people to honor our mission and give all assistance. Sometimes a king will call an assembly of important people and allow us to present our mission. Sometimes, the kings are surrounded by dozens of sub-chiefs and constituents. In one place, the king's men were falling asleep during the gathering. In other places, the people were attentive and communication was strong. In each case, the people sent out a clear message about how much they honor their leader. If we want to know the quality of a leader, we can examine the quality of his assistants.

Similarly, when I notice how nicely people serve their leader, even if I don't know the particular leader, I receive an impression of his power to lead and enthuse his followers. What a leader expresses, his followers will reflect back into the community.

BE PREPARED FOR EVERYTHING

> *"Never trust the guardians of the city or fort implicitly."*

A good ruler is always prepared. He has alternate ideas if his original plan does not succeed. And if something goes wrong he is prepared to deal with it. Because he is so protective and caring, he takes extra precaution in all areas.

ALL THE KING'S MEN

> *"Having performed his twilight devotions, let him, well armed, hear in an inner apartment the doings of those who make secret reports and of his spies."*

The spies should bring the king information about his subjects. It is the king's duty to minimize the sinful activities committed in his kingdom; therefore, it is important that he knows what his subjects are doing. Lord Rama, the incarnation of Krishna described in the *Ramayana* (the ancient Indian epic), considered this duty so important that he disguised himself and entered even the *dhobis'* or laundry men's village. In this way, he discovered what His citizens were thinking. A good leader should be aware of his area of activity, and others as well. In this way he can understand better the real needs of his dependents so he can serve and protect them with full facility.

BE DIRECTLY INVOLVED

> *"Supervise the work of all the officers yourself."*

Again, Bhishma mentions delegation. The king should directly supervise his top officers so that they will feel sufficiently supported and clear about their mission in representing the king. By supervising them directly, he should also empower them to act on his behalf. Otherwise, the delegates may feel hesitant when making decisions. They may not know the leader well enough to understand what direction he would take on a particular issue. If an officer is not sufficiently supported, the people in general will lose faith in his ability to represent the leader.

UNDERSTANDING THE PRINCIPLE OF SELF-INTEREST

> *"Self-interest is the most powerful fact in everyone's life. No one is dear to another unless there is gain involved."*

Leaders understand that self-interest is a powerfully motivating force. If leaders can enthuse others by speaking to their own self-interests, or if they can even be aware that people are motivated by personal desires, there will be less likelihood of failure.

APPROPRIATE PUNISHMENT

> *"Know how to use the powers of punishment and do not hesitate to use them on miscreants. People are often led by chastisement. Know, then, the science of chastisement."*

In leadership, the judicious use of punishment is important. Excessive punishment leads to chaos, but if a leader fails to address the faults of those under him, he will simply help to reinforce those faults and the society will become degraded. It is often difficult, however, to achieve the proper balance.

ENVIRONMENTAL CONCERNS

> *"Pay attention to the state of the kingdom. Old and ramshackle surroundings are a sign of disregard. Renovate to win good opinion."*

When things are neat, clean and organized, a message is sent out that something important is happening. Organized surroundings tell people that there is structure to the project, as well as order and vision. In general, people do not like to be a part of something that seems inherently unsuccessful. Most people prefer to participate in projects that appear progressive. When people feel they are involved in something successful, it is easier for them to commit themselves to working for greater success. That is human nature. If the surroundings say, "Failure, failure, failure," even if we try to assure people that their project will be a success, the environment will speak louder than our words. The surroundings represent the present state of affairs, and most people judge by what is happening in the present, not by what could happen in the future.

Cleanliness and order are also important because we want to remember that everything belongs to God. Order can be used to glorify God, because it can attract people to serve Him. That initial attraction will put them in a position to hear higher philosophy. If we tell people we have a high philosophy but we live at a low standard, they will not be attracted.

PARENTAL MOOD REVISITED

> *"People should live in freedom and happiness as they do in their father's house."*

Again, Bhishmadeva mentions the parental mood. The very essence of the king's role is to protect the people and their happiness. This point is mentioned again and again in scripture. Seeing to the happiness of others is one of the first duties of a king.

> *"It is not easy to secure people's happiness. You must use diverse methods, skills, cleverness, and truth. All these are important."*

Sometimes we unfortunately do not have good relations with our leaders or fathers. If we think our father to be a good person and maintain a good relationship with him, we will feel comfortable in our father's house. We will feel protected, comfortable, and secure. Leaders should help their dependents feel similarly protected—as if they are in their father's house. If within that house they have freedom, protection, and security, they will feel appreciated and loved.

GOOD ASSOCIATION

> *"Surround yourself with people of like nature who have noble qualities. The only difference between the king and the king's officer is the white umbrella signifying a higher office."*

The best leaders are surrounded by powerful people, and this is because they value strength. If leaders want to accomplish great things, they need people around them who are capable of helping them. Good leaders also have the ability to empower others to do things beyond their imagined capacity.

Good leaders want to help others become good leaders, too. A good leader wants to be surrounded by a variety of people, with diverse forms of intelligence, insight and creativity. In this way, they can make their mission strong.

Visionary leadership does not mean that everyone must have the exact same vision of how the mission should be accomplished. What it does mean is that they should all be dedicated to the mission in general. People may have different conceptions about the vision. That cannot be avoided. They should, however, all agree on the goal.

NICE WORDS

> *"Be pleasant in speech."*

Good leaders know how to use words to help others focus on the mission.

THE IMPORTANCE OF CHARACTER

> *"Dharma (religiosity), integrity, right action, and morality are the watch words of a king."*

Nothing is more powerful than *dharma* and integrity. When we fail to follow *dharma*, we lose integrity. Death is approaching each of us at every moment. What we planned to do tomorrow must be done today. Death is ruthless. It will not wait until our projects are complete. Readiness is important. The world is but a passing parade. We are born alone and die alone. We have not a single lasting companion in our march through this incident called life.

> *"The spouse, the mother, the father, the sons, the kinsmen, the friends—all will walk away from our bodies at death to go on with their own work. Only dharma follows the soul."*

After death, when the body is cremated, buried, etc., the survivors turn away from it, leaving it for the empty shell it is. And the soul, no longer encased in the body, travels on, followed only by its integrity, right action, morality, and truthfulness. Bhishmadeva adds, "Truthfulness is the only friend of a man and the only thing he should seek."

After this instruction, Bhishmadeva noticed that the sun was moving toward the north. He stopped speaking, focused his eyes on Krishna's lotus form, and prepared to leave his body.

VISIONARY LEADERSHIP

Before we conclude our discussion on Bhishmadeva's instructions, we want to more closely examine visionary leadership, which Bhishmadeva also so nicely represents. Good leadership is not just a matter of making things happen; it is a matter of making essential things happen, making important and productive things happen, and helping people feel good about what is happening. Leaders need to have a vision, but they also need to know how to convince others that their vision can manifest, and how to empower them to participate in the mission of bringing the vision about.

In order for this to be possible, the vision must be clear. The more clarity we have, the more we will be able to pass that on to others. It does not matter whether we are working in an office, in the garden, or doing some other service—we should be clear about why we are doing what we do. Without clarity, we build upon a faulty foundation. Part of clarity is facing our present situation. If we think we are further along in fulfilling the vision than we are and we try to build from that misconception, our building will be weak.

After facing our present reality, we must investigate our ideals. This is how our mission is defined. We can then decide how to best go about reaching those ideals. That decision becomes our vision.

Leaders must be able to clearly communicate their particular vision of how to accomplish the mission. Followers must be convinced that the leader has a deep, passionate conviction in the correctness of his direction and that all who follow him will benefit. Followers must be excited and energized by the leader's vision. Often leaders use themes, phrases and slogans as *mantras* to help others focus on the vision and to re-energize them. These slogans also help us bond around the same ideas. Those who are transcendentalists know more than others the potency of *mantras* and how they affect consciousness.

A leader must also be prepared to motivate followers in an ongoing way. Sometimes, we have a vision and enthusiasm, but no perseverance—not enough commitment. We may maintain our enthusiasm for a while, but as our enthusiasm wanes, so will the enthusiasm of our followers. If a leader is not enthused, how can he hope to maintain the enthusiasm of others? Enthusiasm cannot be contrived. People consciously or unconsciously know when their leader is genuinely enthused about a project, or when he is working simply out of duty or for some ulterior motive. When the leader is not energized, the people will not be empowered.

Leaders should also strictly avoid deviation. When a leader deviates, it saps the followers' zeal and dampens their faith and dedication. If the followers even think their leaders have deviated, they will be so disturbed that they will not be able to maintain the vision or progress toward their goal.

Therefore, leaders should always be above suspicion. This means that leaders should be free of sin—they should not break basic moral and ethical principles. They should be so strict in their personal behavior that people cannot even imagine them deviating.

Leaders should ask themselves often why they have accepted a leadership role. It is important that they examine their commitment, motivations, and innermost feelings. "Why am I really doing this service? Is it because I want to become famous? Is it because I want others to do my work for me? Is it because I enjoy making others take risks, or that I enjoy experimenting with their lives?"

Always remember that although problems are inevitable, a visionary leader invariably deals with problems in a caring manner.

Our leadership style must instill faith in others. If our vision and enthusiasm are strong but our management style causes others to distrust us, it will become difficult to achieve our goals. Sincere people will follow only as long as they have confidence in our vision. Many alternative communities from around the world have been started, maintained for some time, and then dwindled. Why did they fail? Often because people dedicated themselves to something they thought could be successful, made a leap of faith, and then lost that faith, perhaps becoming doubtful about the very vision itself.

People must be confident that their leader can achieve his ideals, or at least that he will continue striving for them.

To maintain this faith, leaders must display the personal qualities that instill trust, such as courage, competence, decisiveness, teamwork, and impartiality. Leaders should oversee the work but should not become involved in petty disputes. Sometimes leaders lose their credibility by becoming distracted by minor quarrels.

Perhaps it sounds like I am contradicting myself. Leaders should be aware of their followers' feelings through monitoring, and they should be concerned, but when leaders put themselves in situations where they have to deal with pettiness, they lose some of their own effectiveness. As Bhishmadeva explained, leaders should oversee their officers; they should empower others to handle a certain amount of the responsibility though they themselves should remain responsible for the vision.

Therefore, it is important for leaders to be trained. Many successful corporations and organizations have invested time and money in training and maintaining their managers and employees. If they constantly had to train new people while their trusted workers went out the door, they would be subject to diminishing returns. Sometimes these corporations have their managers and employees pledge commitments to serve the company after they have received training.

Part of leadership training is to learn how to recognize the propensities of others. Then, leaders should engage their followers in work that suits their natures and thus inspire and enthuse them to work for the mission. In some cases, leaders may want to refine their vision for enhancing productivity.

In general, leaders should be concerned about working with what one has.

No leader can please everyone. That is not what leadership means. If a leader is strong, those who are lazy or deviant will be most displeased. At the same time, if too many people are disturbed, the leader should take a closer look at how he is working. Bhishmadeva says that leaders should always examine themselves. He also said that they should not be interested in making either enemies or friends. They should neither be too mild nor too fierce. Leaders who try to please everyone are not real leaders.

And leaders who do not lead are not leaders. One who wishes to lead must have both a vision and the faith to move toward it. Leaders who are constantly pushing or dragging people to work for that vision are not leaders. One should lead from the front—by inspiring people with one's own example—rather than from the rear, pushing people from the back.

CONCLUSION

Here we conclude this discussion from the *Mahabharata* epic on Bhishmadeva's instructions to King Yudhisthira, spoken with all the blessings of Krishna Himself. Bhishmadeva conveyed his instructions for the benefit of the entire world. This discussion has value beyond the scope of a conversation on a battlefield, just as Arjuna's conversation with Krishna, resulting in the *Bhagavad-gita*, was spoken so the whole world could be enlightened. This is one of the oldest discussions on leadership known to mankind, and yet it has great value for today.

As applied to our present discussion, Bhishmadeva's teachings offer interesting insights into the spiritual paradigm, directly instructing us how to deal with material energy in such a way that we do not become enslaved or captured by it, or remain in denial about our actual condition. Rather, by studying this conversation we can learn how to become free of material conditioning. In that sense, some Vedic followers feel that the ideas expressed by Bhishmadeva can be more important than most ideas expressed by the world's best thinkers in the best cutting-edge books and seminars. They know that Krishna Himself has approved Bhishmadeva's words. Thus, if our journey toward proper leadership takes heed of these primary instructions, we will find that our lives as visionary servant-leaders will have already begun, and that our spiritual dimension will come to life much more as well.

PART II
SERVANT-LEADERSHIP: PAST AND PRESENT

"The most important human endeavor is the striving for morality in our actions. Our inner balance and even our very existence depend on it. Only morality in our actions can give beauty and dignity to our lives."

-Albert Einstein

QUESTIONS AND ANSWERS
RELATED TO THE RULE OF KING PRITHU

This section relates to the rule of King Prithu, a divine monarch and first class visionary servant-leader mentioned in India's ancient *Srimad-Bhagavatam*. A study of the life of this noble king will help us embrace many useful ideas from ancient universal wisdom while simultaneously empowering us to use secular technologies for the fulfillment of our needs and goals. One does not have to be familiar with the ancient texts to benefit from this presentation; however, I hope this book will encourage readers to further investigate the lives of Bhishma and King Prithu.

LEADERS ARE BORN FROM THE PEOPLE

Q: In this age, people in general consider democracy better than monarchy, mainly because monarchs have tended to abuse their positions and have not properly protected their citizens. Neither have they taken counsel from *brahmanas*. Democracy literally means "rule by the people," and is meant to elect the people's choice to a position of leadership. In these cases, the people either force leaders to come to the lowest common denominator in order to get the vote; or by canvassing people to vote for them, good leaders increase the standard of their constituency. What do you think about this?

A: People need to be trained to recognize excellent leadership; otherwise, they will choose leaders based on unhealthy criteria. They will support leaders who promise to fulfill their sense desires rather than their real physical, emotional and spiritual needs.

Leaders are born from the people. If the people are not trained to recognize good leadership, then good leadership will not manifest among them. Rather, the leaders born of such a society will lack personal integrity and they will support only what makes them popular and gratifies their own senses.

It is important to establish a clear understanding of what constitutes a true leader for our discussion about these two important leaders from ancient Vedic culture.

WHAT MAKES A LEADER?

Managers are fairly common; real leaders are extremely rare. Managers use people to make things happen; leaders make things happen for the people. Managers often lead from the back. They may watch to see what is popular, what seems politically correct, what will help them increase their own status and especially, what will help them increase their incomes. Managers tend to be utilitarian and opportunistic.

True leaders, however, always lead from the front. They are associated with the "four C's:"

- Character
- Competence
- Compassion
- Courage

When we find a true leader, we will find strong performance in all these areas. There are so many definitions for the word "leadership" in the English language alone. Such a diversity of meanings for the same word indicates that people are confused about what it means. It is a complex topic.

The work of a true leader can also be listed in descending order of significance:

- To be
- To do
- To see
- To tell

Similarly, we can categorize citizens in a general way:

- Inventors: Those who make things happen
- Resenters: Those who watch things happen (and often complain about how they are happening)
- Consenters: those who do not know what is happening, but who consent and go with the flow.

True leaders are always inventors. They are experts at making things happen. There are so many analogies to help us understand the qualities of a leader. Here's another one, relating to the attitude people have when they approach a hill:

- There are those who see the hill as an obstacle, and immediately give up their plans.
- There are those who see the hill and decide to camp at its base.
- There are those who see the hill and proceed to climb it.

Those who quit are the types of people who become discouraged by adversity. They do not possess the perseverance, stamina or the deep commitment to attain the goal. Those who camp at the hill's base may start off with enthusiasm, but they become distracted by the obstacle and lose sight of the goal. Those who climb the hill despite the promise of difficulty have enough commitment to work for success. Their challenge is to maintain their vision and sense of mission, and by continuing to strive, they can achieve their goal.

Retired United States Army General Norman Schwarzkopf said in his analysis of losers vs. winners:

- To a loser, it may be possible, but it is difficult.
- To a winner, it may be difficult, but it is possible.
- A leader says that nothing is impossible.
- A loser will say: "It's not my job."
- A winner will say: "Let me help you do it."
- A leader will say: "Follow me and do as I do."

Others have categorized people into winners and whiners. One should live one's life by discipline, not emotion.

- Winners, and especially true leaders, feel good when they do right.
- Whiners must feel good before they will do right.
- Winners say: "I will do it because it is right, and I will feel good knowing I acted properly."
- Whiners say: "If I ever feel good about it, then I will do it."
- Winners say: "I must believe it before I can see it."
- Whiners say: "I must see it before can I believe it."

True leaders know that progress is motivating; apparent progress based on lust, greed and self-deception is actually failure.

True leaders make things happen, are winners, lead from the front and always keep the highest welfare of their constituents in mind. In this way, a leader will inspire people to come to a higher standard by their own superior qualities.

HIGHLIGHTS OF A TRUE LEADER'S CHARACTER

I like to think of a true leader not simply as a person who leads but as a servant-leader. In Sanskrit, a servant is called *dasanudasa*, literally, "a servant of the servant." This is definitely the quality of a servant-leader. He serves his constituents, who are themselves engaged in various occupations and professions, where they render and receive all kinds of services.

A servant-leader is interested in stewardship. He sees himself as a caretaker rather than as a proprietor or dictator.

A servant-leader has a passion to serve others. In that sense, he is leading, but mainly helping to guarantee that goals will be met. Instead of waiting for someone else to do the needful, a servant-leader will step to the front and do it himself, especially when the people's welfare is at stake. A true servant-leader does not become addicted to privilege. Rather, the more assets and privileges he obtains, the more humble and responsible a servant-leader becomes. We consistently see that a servant-leader has a healthy possession of power, which he uses to increase his or her responsibility and to facilitate the achievement of his goals.

When a servant-leader is served, he himself becomes a better servant. The more influence and facility a servant-leader has, the more he uses them to give back to the people. A servant-leader is always a good listener, is empathetic and looks constantly for ways to bring healing and nurturing to all situations that appear "broken" or in conflict. A servant-leader is aware of what is going on around him. He is also persuasive, sharing his ideas with others and building stronger communities.

TEN CHARACTERISTICS OF A SERVANT-LEADER

1. **A servant-leader is a deep lover of people**

    In Sanskrit we say *param-duhkha-duhkhi krpam buddhi*. This means that a servant-leader feels the suffering of others, because he is in tune with his constituents and genuinely concerned for their welfare. A servant-leader's empathy is genuine.

A servant-leader has a great appreciation for power, money, facility and any other type of asset—not because he sees himself as a proprietor, but because he understands that such facility is necessary to become genuinely productive. A servant-leader feels a passion to help others, but realizes that if he has no facility to do so, his passion will not be realized. A servant-leader loves power, influence, money and assets, but simply to coordinate their use for the benefit of the people under his care.

King Prithu is an example of such a leader. He states:

> *"The King will respect all women as if they were his own mother, and he will treat his own wife as the other half of his body. He will be just like an affectionate father to his citizens, and he will treat himself as the most obedient servant of the devotees, who always preach the glories of the Lord."*
>
> **-Srimad-Bhagavatam, 4.16.17**

Later, in the commentary to another verse, we find:

> *Prithu Maharaja was also very humble, meek and gentle, and whenever he performed any philanthropic work or welfare activity for the general public, he would labor exactly as if he were tending to his own personal necessities. In other words, his philanthropic activities were not for the sake of show but were performed out of personal feeling and commitment. All philanthropic activities should be thus performed.*[4]

The late John D. Rockefeller is remembered as a contemporary leader who displayed servant-leader qualities, even if, in other areas, he was a bit controversial. He said repeatedly, "God gave me my money, He favored me because He knew I would give it back." In this area, John D. Rockefeller walked his talk. From his first boyhood job, he donated 6 percent of his wages to charity. By the time he was twenty, he had surpassed the 10 percent mark. When he died at ninety-seven, he had given away most of his money to build countless hospitals, churches, museums and educational institutions. His life was an example of stewardship. He saw that God had arranged for him to have so much, so that he could help others.

2. A servant-leader helps people feel happy and secure

Too many people in society are disturbed. They feel unprotected, insecure and unhappy. A servant-leader

---
[4] Swami Prabhupada, *Srimad-Bhagavatam*, 4.22.62 purport

is sensitive to what people are feeling. When an empowered servant-leader is in charge, there can never be rampant misery.

A servant-leader is attuned to people's needs and the resolution of conflicts. In Sanskrit, this is referred to as *sarve sukhino bhavantu*. This also means that a servant-leader skillfully deflects misfortune. We should also note how important it is for the people in modern society to feel happy, secure, protected and loved. With the globalization of markets and the increase of technological capacities, it is becoming more and more important for leaders, managers, and CEOs to produce things inexpensively, quickly and with greater quality. The competition between companies is so intense that what often determines corporate survival is a corporation's ability to empower its employees in "team playing." Empowering employees and creating healthy teams is based almost entirely on people feeling good about themselves, about others, about the institutions or corporations for which they work, about the leaders of those institutions and especially about the mission or vision associated with both their leaders and the institutions for which they work.

A few years ago, I spoke at the annual convention of the National American Medical Association, Family Practice division. In my speech, I particularly emphasized the power of love, of happiness and of a sense of security. I explained how all those things have a positive effect on the hypothalamus. The hypothalamus is a gland that regulates such things as sleep patterns, body temperature and the release of hormones from the pituitary gland. In many ways, the hypothalamus affects the health of the entire body. When someone is feeling good about themselves, the hypothalamus regulates the body in a healthy way; when they are not feeling good about themselves or their environment, and are feeling anxious, then the hypothalamus responds by stimulating the body in negative ways. Mental anxiety is often channeled by neurotransmitters and delivered to various parts of the body. It can be said that the mind is actually attacking the body. Every physical illness has a mental counterpart. Louise L. Hay's teachings, as well as her book, *Heal Your Body*, clearly explain the mental causes for physical illness, and the transformational tools to overcome them.

Let us offer an additional way of looking at hormonal influence. Love and positive emotions release endorphins in the blood. Endorphins are the body's natural painkillers and they strengthen the immune system. Conversely negative emotions, worry, anger, depression, etc. dump high levels of adrenaline into the blood. Adrenaline constricts blood vessels and raises blood pressure. So the more we have gratitude, feel love, etc. the more endorphins and less adrenaline we deposit in our bodies. As we count our blessings we literally bathe ourselves in good hormones.

Studies in psycho-neural immunology and psychosomatic disease also help us to understand the powers that affect the body. Peter R. Schemm, Ph.D., wrote a wonderful book, entitled *Love: Impact on Physical and Mental Health*. He explains that people who live in relationships in which they do not feel loved, protected, happy or secure are ten times more susceptible to chronic disease and five times more susceptible to mental illness. Dr. Dean Ornish, MD, makes a similar point in his book, *Love and Survival*. He points out the scientific basis for the healing power of love and emotional intimacy. In his studies, he found that one who does not feel loved is three to five times more susceptible to disease or premature death. His studies prove that love heals.

In a conference on health held in Philadelphia in March 2001, I had the opportunity to present a paper on spirituality and health. I discussed numerous studies proving that religious faith and practices help in facing, accepting and curing all types of disease. One study showed that women who give birth with the support of a loved one need less anesthesia and have less incidence of cesarean deliveries. The bottom line is that people can avoid illness, heal better from illnesses they already have and become more productive in all areas of their lives if they feel loved, secure and happy about themselves and their environment.

Many years ago, I worked on stress and time management among diplomats at the United Nations in Geneva. I was amazed to see how many diplomats were suffering from illness, having accidents or being forced into early retirement due to excessive stress. I found that it often stemmed from their not feeling happy about themselves or their environment. In some cases, they were disturbed with their family lives or with world problems in general. In the 1990s I had a conversation with the then-president of Nigeria, General Obansenjo. He shared with me a story about his past, when he was living in an opulent suburb of England. He said he had become discouraged living there because the neighbors were impersonal and distant. He told me that his next-door neighbor's husband died, and it took him weeks to find out there had been a death in the family. He commented that Western society emphasizes individualism, rapid growth and material development rather than community, and that this has caused people to lose touch with themselves, to develop low self-esteem, and to also lose touch with others. Community is based on sharing and concern for one another. If we do not reach out even when we are in distress, we must indeed be very much alone. A good leader will not allow such social and personal disintegration, but will implement policies that engender a sense of community, security and protection.

3. **A servant-leader creates lasting value**

   In order to determine how to best move forward, a servant-leader learns from the past and looks carefully at the present before moving into what he hopes will be a brighter future. A servant-leader is not concerned with short-term success for his constituents, nor is he concerned with personal success. Rather, he is inspired by an idea or vision higher than himself. In this way, he will achieve enduring results. One who is fixated on short-term success will not be able to create enduring results for all involved. In Sanskrit this short-term success is called *preyas* and the lasting, enduring results that have ultimate value are referred to as *sreyas*.

   There is an East African proverb that states that while we may think we have inherited the present from our ancestors, we have actually borrowed it from our future, our children. A servant-leader understands that what we do now will influence how our children will live their lives. Our children will have to live with the results of our current activities. A servant-leader, therefore, thinks about how to live in the present so that the future will have more value. He does not want to leave our children with nothing after he and his constituents have misused and abused the resources that were available during his time.

   In his book, *When Your Customer Wins, You Can't Lose*, Jack Collins makes some important points about the importance of a client or member of an institution feeling valued. He breaks down into percentages the reasons why a person will separate himself from a company or institution: Nine percent of the people will leave because the competition has offered them a better deal. Fourteen percent of the people will leave because of product (or institutional) dissatisfaction. In contrast, 75 percent of people will leave because they feel devalued or unappreciated. These people stay away from the institution, while the others may come back in due course.

His point is that people naturally align themselves with institutions, organizations or products. Seventy-five percent of them will remain despite more tempting offers from the competition or some product dissatisfaction simply because they feel they are valued. He adds that a typical, dissatisfied customer will tell eight to ten others about their dissatisfaction. Such dissatisfied customers become bad public relations for the corporation or institution. Only 5 percent of the people who separate themselves from a business or institution will complain directly to the organization; 70 percent of the dissatisfied clients will complain to others. It is also quite likely that those who hear the complaint will accept the dissatisfied customer's perception and will trust his or her opinion. Those who hear the complaints are unlikely to ever try the product. Bad news always travels faster than good news. Good news rarely overtakes bad news.

Success in business is based on the quality of the relationship between the corporation and its clients. It costs six times as much to attract a new customer as it does to maintain an existing one, and when we lose a client, we are actually losing eight to ten potential clients—those who will accept the dissatisfied client's complaint as accurate. If we lose a participant in the business—an employee or manager—we lose all our training investment and the expertise he or she has developed. An organization cannot really be successful if it continually loses either members or clients.

There is a wonderful book edited by Marshall Goldsmith, Lawrence Lyons, and Alyssa Freeas, called *Coaching For Leadership*, which states that when someone assumes a new leadership role today, he or she has a 40 percent chance of demonstrating disappointing performance, voluntarily leaving or being fired within twelve to eighteen months. That is, a new leader has a 40 percent chance of being unsuccessful. Not only will we have wasted time and money on training such a person, but we also may be eliminating our pool of potential candidates as the dissatisfied trainee complains about us to others. Why do these people fail? The editors explain that 82 percent of them fail to build partnership and teamwork relationships with subordinates and peers; 58 percent are confused or unclear about what is expected of them; and 50 percent lack the required internal politics or skills and knowledge to be able to be successful. Thus we see how important it is that each person feels properly valued so that they can stay in the organization or institution and use what they have learned for the ultimate success of the enterprise.

In the words of Jeremy Rifkin's *The Age of Access*:

> *In the early periods of capitalism emphasis was on selling goods and services. In the age of access with the cyberspace economy, the commodification of goods and services becomes secondary to the commodification of human relationships. Holding clients and customers attention and pleasing them is essential. Success in the new era will belong to those who are able to make the transition from a production to a marketing perspective, from the notion of making sales to establishing relationships.*

The old way was to sell to as many customers as possible; the new way is to sell as much to each customer as possible, maintaining the relationship over a long period of time, and by carrying a variety of products. Rifkin explains the importance of pleasing the customer for life. He explains, for example, that the average loyal supermarket customer is worth about $4,000 a year. The average new customer at a Cadillac dealership represents a potential lifetime value of more than $322,000. This figure is a projection of the automobiles and service the customer is likely to purchase over time. In this case, we see that the key is to find the appropriate means to hold on to the customer for life. This requires that we must actually value the customer, who will reciprocate by buying our product. When we value the customer and create value for the customer, then the customer will value his collective stewardship with the company and together create long-term value.

4. A servant-leader is a philosopher

A servant-leader always seeks truth and *dharma*. As previously mentioned, *dharma* is a difficult word to define in English because the Sanskrit word has so many subtleties. *Dharma* refers to religion, ethics, integrity, truth, and ultimately to all things in the eternal realm (*sanatana-dharma*). A servant-leader is a philosopher because every leader with higher consciousness is to some degree engaged in philosophy and searching for true essence and meaning, and they are constantly trying to understand underlying truths. A servant-leader should see truth and give himself fully to the pursuit of truth without being intimidated or deterred.

Seeking truth means to seek out the inner relatedness of all things. Seeking truth requires the willingness to ask questions that take us beyond our usual business, political, religious or ethical interests to see a greater picture. It means studying the full consequences of our actions. Typical questions of a truth-seeking servant-leader: What is real? What is universal? Who will benefit by what I am proposing to do? Who will be harmed by what I am proposing to do? What is power? What is security? What is success? What is wealth? What is love? What will death mean to my ambitions? (These questions are discussed in the first book in my *Leadership for an Age of Higher Consciousness* series: *Administration from a Metaphysical Perspective*.)

Upon discovering higher truths through research and self-examination, one should always know that there is more to explore and understand. One who is seeking higher truths should never feel satisfied with what he has discovered. The more we understand, the more we realize how little we know compared to the vast world of knowledge and experience. Thus a servant-leader remains open-minded and constantly aware of stewardship, despite any apparent power he may have.

When it is time to make decisions, a truth-seeking servant-leader will do so. When it is time to commit, a truth-seeking servant-leader will do so. When it is time to act, a truth-seeking servant-leader will do so. But a true servant-leader will never stop seeking higher truths.

5. A servant-leader leads from the inside out

A servant-leader develops his character. Good character, or integrity, is power. In Sanskrit, we call this *acara* and *pracara*. *Acara* means behavior, and *pracara* literally means "teachings" or words. Both a leader's words and actions should be exemplary. This exemplary good character is called *sadacara*.

As we have previously discussed, in the late 1980s and early 1990s, the American government began to study why Japanese businesses were so much more successful than American businesses, even though Americans had better schools and more facility. Stanford University spent millions of dollars to study this phenomenon.

The researchers discovered that it had more to do with the Japanese mentality than American ingenuity. The Japanese have more of a family culture. Even in the business world, employers and managers work together better, communicate better, and tend to understand the inside workings of things better than Americans. Their success was based on their closer relationships. The Japanese tended not to see themselves as working for a company but that they are part of the company. Thus they are more willing to share collectively in a company's successes or failures. They were also more empowered individually in their work, because their companies were built on teamship, relationships, and especially, character. American business schools now teach that management success is about 20 percent technique and 80 percent relationship. Relationship, of course, means understanding people's needs and being able to lead more from the inside out—from a platform of strong character.

Leading from the outside-in means that everything is based on productivity and the other externals of business. Many organizations, businesses and corporations are literally being forced to work at healthier communication in order to survive. Without a culture of caring, there is no hope for world-class achievement. Japan's success is based on the *bushido* and *samurai* culture—the culture of duty, sacrifice, humility and hard work. Where character is strong, there will be a constant desire to become uplifted in all aspects of life. Strong character means a strong sense of morality in all areas of one's life. As Gandhi said, "A person cannot do right in one department of life while attempting to do wrong in another department. Life is one indivisible whole."

In 1998, when President Clinton was under scrutiny for his illicit relationship in the White House, the editor of the Religion section of the *Washington Post* asked me to offer a message for Valentine's Day about integrity and principle-centered leadership. In my message to the American citizens, I stressed that a leader's private and public lives should be consistent, and I explained some of the principles of servant-leadership. Servant-leaders understand that while knowledge gives power, character is power. Again, a servant-leader leads from the inside out. Over the last thirty years I have had several opportunities to meet with CEOs of many corporations, leaders of religious institutions, and presidents of countries, and have had the chance to address the importance of character and of leading from the inside out. Only by developing his own character can a servant-leader be in higher consciousness and help raise the consciousness of his dependents. A leader possessing higher consciousness will manifest excellent character, greater competence, compassion and courage as he or she is being divinely inspired.

Kevin Cashman, in his wonderful book, *Leadership from the Inside Out*, writes:

Most business strategies need to be turned inside out to keep pace with our changing world. Our views of leadership need to be transformed to deal with today's dynamic realities. Much of today's leadership is tactical and specific, focusing on external manifestations such as vision, drive, creativity or charisma. However, these outside factors cannot capture the essence of leadership. Leadership is something deeper, more fundamental. As much as we may try to separate leadership from the person, the two are totally inseparable.

6. A servant-leader is principle-centered

The need for servant-leaders is universal in every culture. In Sanskrit, the words *karma, jnana, vijnana,* and *atmavidya* are used to describe these laws and principles. *Karma* relates to the law of reciprocity, *jnana* to the principle knowledge, *vijnana* to realized knowledge, and *atmavidya* to self-realization, or the understanding of the self as the soul. Understanding these laws and principles creates fairness, integrity, honesty, dignity, service, liberation, love, etc.

One cannot really talk about servant-leadership or about leading from the inside out without addressing the importance of these principles, because principles have to do with ethics. Principles are natural rules whose essence is not subject to relative change. Today's societies, families, institutions and other such systems tend to minimize or deny the importance of universal principles. They find it difficult to be productive and harmonious because they minimize the importance of character development. When we work on developing our sense of justice, honesty and personal integrity we are better able to respect others, even if they are different from us. Without developing ourselves in these ways we will always find diversity to be a reason for conflict. To respect diversity, we have to see the universality of human nature. By focusing on that universality, we can actually celebrate diversity and engender a sense of unity within diversity. This produces synergy. Stephen Covey, in his national bestseller, *Seven Habits of Highly Effective People*, discusses how principles are not the same as values; they are much more binding. He writes that principles apply to individuals, marriages, families and private and public organizations of every kind, and that when the truths are internalized into habits, they empower people.

As we focus on principles, we are able to focus on improving our quality of life. We grow and change, and this is always auspicious. When we focus on principles, we understand the consequences of our activities better. Focusing on principles and universal laws allows us to take a more meaningful approach to life. We become more sensitive and accountable.

A servant-leader focuses on principles and universal laws. This is good for everyone because it creates mutual and personal accountability. When leadership is based on principles and universal laws, trust develops between the leader and his constituents, and when there is trust, projects can become successful both externally and internally.

I was in Ghana in the 1980s, and had been sharing different books with then-president Rawlings. At one point, while Ghana was suffering an internal crisis, I heard that President Rawlings had gathered the heads of all the major religious institutions and criticized them for emphasizing too much the fear of God rather than His love. When I heard this, I understood that our teachings were helping him, because some of the writings I had given him emphasized the higher aspect of love of God. When we fear God or even our human authorities, we may do what is required of us, but we will not act out of love. We act out of understanding and love when we feel the love reciprocated. When we give our best in this type of relationship, we become far more empowered and, of course, happier in our work.

It is essential to develop the principles of compassion, selflessness and love—these are more important than external success and productivity. If there are good relationships, based on higher principles, then there will be success. If not, the laws of reciprocity (*karma*) will affect us and our institutions in a negative way. As both the law of physics and the law of *karma* emphasize, every action has an equal and opposite reaction. The *Bible* states that we reap what we sow. What we "plant" into the environment with our attitudes and actions, we will receive back in equal measure. In *Principle-centered Leadership*, Covey gives one of the nicest definitions of principles:

> *Principles are not invented by us or society, they are laws of the universe pertaining to human relationships and organizations. They are part of the human condition. Examples are fairness, equity, justice, integrity, honesty and trust. They bring stability. When not active they bring disintegration and destruction.*

7. A servant-leader is a powerful visionary

Such a leader must have a powerful and piercing vision with which he can clearly see how to make the best use of his resources. A study of the classic writings on leadership, psychology and spirituality, especially those from the ancient cultures, will help to develop such a vision. In Vedic culture, the topmost visionary is called a *sastra-caksusa*—one who visualizes all things with the aid of the authorized religious scriptures.

A visionary leader seeks to empower others. They continue to search for truth while maintaining their principle-centered focus. Visionary leaders have a good balance between right-brain and left-brain thinking. The right brain is more feminine, nurturing, intuitive and creative; the left-brain is more masculine and "physical," interested more in results. Visionary leaders often produce a host of solutions for social, economic and other types of problems.

If we want visionary leaders, we must, of course, learn to recognize them and support them. Visionary leaders have great qualities, which they develop through their interest in values, intuition and partnership with others. They can bring spiritual culture to our religious and political lives. Mahatma Gandhi once said, "I must first be the change I want to see in my world." A visionary leader knows he must lead by example, and that his leadership will have a powerful impact on both present and future generations.

Visionary leaders honor the inner connection of all life. They recognize that there is a supreme order and that there are inherent and universal needs. Such vision promotes a spirit of trust, partnership and shared vision. They are focused on whole systems in relationship to sustainable development. Such leaders have no problem sacrificing short-term goals for long-term benefits. They stimulate healing rather than attacking problems. They often realize what former UN Secretary General U. Thant once said: "We will not have peace on the planet until we have a spiritual renaissance." Spirituality is not just a matter of religion but is the deeper essence and connection between humanity and the Godhead. Spirituality is the source of the universal principles we have mentioned.

Visionary leaders raise consciousness and inspire people to sacrifice for the greater good. They have a clear vision of the future and the need to transform old paradigms that are no longer relevant. They focus on opportunity rather than problems. They often see problems as chances to embrace a miracle, and they consistently pursue a win-win scheme.

At this point, it should be obvious that the world is in dire need of more visionary leaders. Most major crises in leadership are due to a lack of visionary leadership.

8. A servant-leader keeps everyone engaged according to their propensities

In Sanskrit, we call these propensities *varnas*, all of which function under the modes of nature: goodness, passion and ignorance. Our propensities are determined by our state of consciousness, our occupational capabilities and our spiritual orientation. Those in the mode of goodness tend to be powerful through humility. They are clean, selfless and pure. Those in the mode of passion tend to be selfish, greedy and lusty. Those in the mode of ignorance are lazy, unclean and even obnoxious. Most of us embody a mixture of these attributes as the various modes of nature work on our minds. Servant-leaders understand how the modes act upon individuals, and know that people are different in character, habits, needs and desires based on how they are influenced by the modes. He will then try to engage people in ways that are natural to them and inspire them. If someone has a particular propensity but is not employed accordingly, he is unlikely to be as inspired as if he could work according to his nature.

There are four main *varnas* described in the ancient Vedic

scriptures: *brahmana, ksatriya, vaisya* and *sudra*. The brahminical persons are intellectual and priestly, and will be most inclined to engage in pursuits that emphasize those characteristics. The *ksatriya* leans toward administration, diplomacy and warfare, and is most valuable to society when engaged in these types of work. The *vaisya* likes mercantile activities and farming, and will be most enthused when engaged in this work. A *sudra* is basically a simple person who serves others. They are happiest when engaged in physical work, and when they have been given clear instructions and boundaries about what is and what is not to be done. People feel better about themselves when they are employed according to their own propensities.

Aside from occupational propensities, the *Vedas* describe four spiritual stages of life (*ashramas*): *brahmacari* (celibate student life), *grhastha* (married and raising a family), *vanaprastha* (retired life, where one's children are grown and business activities may begin to diminish), and *sannyasa* (the life of renunciation from family life in order to pursue spiritual goals).

This Vedic system is known as *varnasrama-dharma*, a combination of social and spiritual designations that are meant to engage people according to their natural inclinations. A servant-leader not only understands the importance of *varna* and *ashrama*, but understands that people should be taught to honor God and respect the material energy. In this way, his constituents can be employed in what they feel is meaningful work while enjoying a healthy family and social life. By being taught to concentrate on God, they are empowered to raise their consciousness and to understand the higher goals of life.

Organizations often experience problems because their employees are either not qualified or have little propensity for the positions in which they are employed. They may have no desire to work in the ways in which they are being asked. Sometimes such people even sabotage the operations, consciously or unconsciously. A servant-leader is therefore aware of the psychology of working with people's propensities, and he values everyone according to who they are. From that position, he is able to find the means to help them work in a complementary way or to find them appropriate engagements or employment elsewhere. The *Srimad-Bhagavatam* explains how King Prithu oversaw his citizens as a father cares for his children. The *Manu-samhita* mentions that a leader should know his constituents as well as a mother knows her children and should care for them with the same affection. A servant-leader who does not build a strong culture of trust will not be able to engage his dependents effectively. Therefore, his organization will experience lower productivity.

A friend of mine at the UN once mentioned that he knew a president of a university business school who could understand his students' propensities. He found an interesting way to encourage them in their budding careers. When each student graduated, he gave them a $10,000 grant toward the founding of their new businesses. As years passed, many of his students became successful businessmen. They remembered the start they were given by their old professor and because they felt like valued sons, donated literally millions of dollars to the school they had attended. This university president was obviously both a clever and caring servant-leader, who understood the process of loving reciprocation.

A servant-leader who engages people according to their propensities understands how to satisfy their needs. A servant-leader strives to satisfy needs rather than wants. The fulfillment of needs will satisfy people; the fulfillment of wants will not.

<u>People Want........People Need</u>
Sympathy............empathy
riches...................fulfillment
fame ....appreciation
power..................support and opportunity
domination ....protection
prestige ....recognition and acceptance
freedom ....good guidance and facility
intoxication ....altered awareness and self-actualization

A servant-leader will constantly address others' needs, especially their need for self-actualization and realization, thus helping people to become greater than they could have ever dreamed.

9. A servant-leader is an expert in delegation and empowerment

An organization is effective when its members feel they have a defined and important role to play in its success. Delegation allows this to happen. It is a principle of management that people will work harder to carry out a vision when they have helped to create that vision. When they are key participants, they will feel integral parts of the vision's success.

Tasks can be delegated either in a linear management structure or a matrix structure. A linear management structure works by delegating tasks from the top down, whereas a matrix management structure focuses on particular areas and delegates tasks in an activity-oriented way, as explained in the earlier Bhishma section of this book.

Accountability, however, cannot be delegated. Often, when a leader assigns a task, he attempts to delegate accountability for it too. This is not good delegation. Good delegation means that everyone has a share in the discussion; bad delegation means that everyone is at the mercy of a powerful and sometimes incompetent autocrat. Work can be delegated, but the ultimate accountability must continue to belong to the leader, the person responsible for the delegation.

Good delegation means that the task is well defined. Everyone has a share in the discussion and all parties maintain and honor their accountability. Bad delegation can sometimes come about when tasks are not clearly defined, the resources inadequate, or all parties do not maintain accountability. Worse still is when a manager is an incompetent autocrat who is reluctant to delegate or who delegates poorly because he doesn't sufficiently value or empower others. This is often the case when a leader has too much confidence or pride.

When we delegate, it encourages others to develop their skills as they take personal responsibility for certain tasks. It also allows a leader to choose the person best suited for the job, rather than relying solely upon himself. Offering promotions can also help people develop new skills. Good managers, therefore, always maintain a pool of trained workers who are ready to be promoted to a higher level of responsibility.

Sometimes managers are afraid to delegate responsibility because they are afraid to lose power, control or status. They think that others will see them as less capable in the tasks at hand. Other times, such managers do not delegate responsibility because they are afraid that those to whom they give responsibility will fail. If this happens, not only would the task be returned to them, but they may also have to rectify mistakes already committed. Some so-called leaders think it is easier, therefore, to struggle to complete all tasks themselves.

But when we do not delegate responsibility, we tend to wear ourselves out, which brings up another point about appropriate delegation: Delegation does not mean passing stress onto others along with a given task. Apathetic, unmotivated or overworked staff tends to sabotage a project. If workers feel uninvolved, their energies will not be focused. Their lack of focus will disturb the project's ultimate development. If we do not delegate responsibility, personal duties may actually overlap in different workers' minds, and that can lead to confusion and even hostility. Tasks need to be clearly defined, and appointed to the right people.

Of course, the opposite danger lies in not delegating tasks properly. In this case, no one knows what they are supposed to do, and the tasks become "no one's" responsibility. Again, for such reasons, it is important that tasks be clearly defined and delegated in a responsible manner.

After a task has been delegated, a leader must continue to monitor those to whom the task has been given and maintain the same degree of accountability as if he were doing the work himself. Asking those under him to give regular reports helps in this regard.

A leader must also provide his workers with the proper resources to complete the task. He should at least inform them about how they might acquire these resources themselves.

In his book, *Developing the Leaders Around You*, John Maxwell defines four categories of leaders:

- The Competitor
- The Personal Achiever
- The Team Player
- The Team Builder

He explains that if you can accomplish everything you want to accomplish alone, your dreams are too small. One, he says, is too small a number to produce greatness. Great leaders do great things by helping others also become great. Actually, the sign of a great leader is that he does great things for others.

10. A servant-leader leaves behind a culture of enduring excellence

In the Vedic culture we refer to this as *parampara*, which is an enduring chain of the highest quality of leadership. All great servant-leaders leave a legacy.

Why does a servant-leader care to leave a legacy? Because he loves the people, and he wants to help others follow his good example of using money, power and other assets for the good of the people. He wants to help the people feel happy and secure, to help others value the people, to become philosophers and to search for truth without intimidation, to lead from the inside out. Servant-leaders have dynamic visions that they do not want to see die with them. They want their visions to expand and grow and to continue to enthuse others.

Servant-leaders protect their legacy by acknowledging people's propensities and engaging them accordingly. A servant-leader knows that when people are sufficiently encouraged and empowered, they will, in turn, empower others who work with them and who come after them. The culture of enduring excellence is based on a continual progression of people empowering and enthusing others based on principle-centered leadership.

The servant-leader leaves a powerful legacy because of the following abilities:

- Ability to restructure: Servant-leaders are able to adjust to changes in both technology and in the competition; changes that render previous modes of operating obsolete.
- Ability to allocate resources and set priorities.
- Ability to reengineer, eliminate excess and make processes more efficient.
- Ability to re-invent and constantly ask: "What should I do more of? What should I do less of?"

As a servant-leader wants to leave a legacy, he also wants to live out a legacy. Quality leaders create environments in which a wonderful chain of leaders invariably follow and offer the highest value to the members of the organization. In the Vedic conception, this powerful chain is called *parampara*. The *parampara* is always based on leading from the inside out, and it helps empower people to realize divine goals while facing the usual material problems and achievements.

FINDING COMMON GROUND

Q: Democracy is meant to provide people with a voice in choosing their leaders, which allows them to meet on some sort of common ground. In Vedic culture, the "common ground" was formed by the *varnasrama* institution. Like today, the people were not all the same, still, *varnasrama* provided an institution through which people could voice their needs and legitimate claims as citizens. The *varnasrama* divisions are no longer institutionalized, but they are part of the human psyche, because the system was designed by God and because people are conditioned by the modes. If there is no divine monarch to hear people's needs under the various modes, then democracy seems to provide the common ground. Do you agree?

A: Some of the worst leaders in world history have been autocrats and tyrants who misused autocratic power and abused their constituents. However, it can also be said that some of the world's greatest leaders have been monarchs. Powerful government systems can either bring great rewards or great harm to the people. When misused, kingship can bring disaster. Because the monarch has such total power, he can devastate his country or uplift and energize it.

In ancient Vedic times, the monarch was considered *naradeva*—God represented in human form. In other words, the king was accepted as God's direct representative. The divine monarch was empowered by God and would be offered all assistance and facility by the demigods—agents even more powerful than angels and archangels. The king worked simultaneously from the platforms of material, metaphysical and spiritual power, and was imbued with purity and genuine concern for his people. The *Srimad-Bhagavatam* explains that divine monarchs possessed eight mystic opulences (*siddhis*). These eight perfections were *anima*, the power to decrease in size and to enter an atom; or to become lighter than a feather; *mahima*, the power to make oneself very heavy or very large; *laghima*, the power to travel to other planets; *prapti*, the power of acquisition; *isita*, the power to create or destroy a planet; *vasita*, the power of mind-control and hypnosis; *prakamya*, various types of magic within the scope of nature; and *kamavasayita*, mystic power that transcended the laws of nature.

India's ancient texts contain a thorough explanation of these eight mystic perfections, and also mention ten secondary and five inferior perfections.[5] The divine monarch possessed these eight mystic perfections and, in addition, was given special protection and blessings by the demigods. From this alone we can understand why divine monarchy is out of the question in the twenty-first century. Where would we find such a monarch?

But let us look a little closer at some of the qualities a divine monarch would possess. By recognizing and emulating some of these qualities, today's leaders can come to a higher level of excellence.

---

5   Swami Prabhupada, *Srimad-Bhagavatam*, 11.15.4-5

QUALITIES OF DIVINE MONARCHS

The Fourth Canto of the *Srimad-Bhagavatam* explains that a king would sacrifice his personal convenience to serve his citizens. He had a deep love for his people, and was as affectionate as a father. He also knew his subjects as a mother would know her children, and would care for them with that same kind of intense affection. The Fourth Canto also discusses how a king would perform welfare activities as if they were his personal necessities. In his commentary on *Srimad-Bhagavatam*, 5.7.4, A.C. Bhaktivedanta Swami states:

> *Although formerly the government was a monarchy, all of the kings were very affectionate toward their citizens and they strictly kept them engaged in their respective duties. Therefore society was very smoothly conducted.*

The key concepts here are that kings were affectionate and that they engaged people in their respective duties. That is, a divine monarch was not a tyrant but the greatest example of a servant-leader. In the wonderful epic, *Ramayana*, Rama instructs his brother Bharata:

> *It comes to you as your natural duty to secure peace and happiness for the inhabitants of your kingdom. A load rests on his shoulders who takes from his subjects one sixth of their belongings but protects them not as the very children of his loins. Boundless fame to the end of time, crown him who seeks the welfare of his people with unflagging care and zeal as he would his life and that of his children, dearer to him than life.*

The *Bhagavatam* tells us that the king could collect taxes. However, the taxes were not meant only to line his own coffers; he was meant to spend the taxes on the citizens in ways that would benefit them, and he was personally responsible to oversee their protection if an emergency arose.

From A.C. Bhaktivedanta Swami's purport to *Srimad-Bhagavatam*, 3.16.10:

> Those who are helpless must be taken care of by their respective guardians. Otherwise the guardian will be subjected to the punishment of Yamaraja, who is appointed by the Lord to supervise the activities of the sinful living creatures. The assistants or messengers of Yamaraja are likened here to vultures, and those who do not execute their respective duties in protecting their wards are compared to serpents. Vultures deal very seriously with serpents, and similarly the messengers will deal very seriously with neglectful guardians.

From the purport to *Srimad-Bhagavatam*, 4.9.65-67:

> Although it is misconceived that formerly a monarchal government was autocratic, from the description of this verse it appears that not only was King Uttanapada a rajarsi, but before installing his beloved son Dhruva on the throne, he consulted his officers, considered the opinion of the public and also personally examined Dhruva's character.

Also:

> *Formerly this earth was ruled by only one saintly king. Kings were trained to become saintly. Therefore they would know the concerns and the welfare of the citizens.*

These points are all significant. Uttanapada, the father of Dhruva, was a powerful king, but when he wanted to enthrone his son Dhruva, he did not make the decision autocratically. First he sought the approval of his ministers, then the people, and only then did he personally examine his son's character to see if his son was actually fit to rule. The order of these steps is also important. A king's ministers are supposed to know both what the people need and what is needed for the smooth management of the empire. The people should also be petitioned. How do they see his son? Accepting their recommendations, the king is then free to apply his own criteria to his son's character and to test his strength, courage, wisdom and generosity. Only after all three of these stages were completed did he consider placing his son on the throne.

Kings were particularly trained to become saintly and to have no concern beyond the welfare of their citizens. This mentality is the qualification of a divine monarch. The monarch was trained systematically to care for his citizens' needs. This was his *raison d'etre*. In fact, the essence of a divine monarch was his position as the topmost servant-leader, one who had no concern other than to facilitate, protect and guide his citizens. Those who served under such a monarch were extremely blessed.

Here are some of the duties of a divine monarch:

- *Dosana*: to see that there is sufficient food to feed all of the citizens.
- *Prinama*: distributing gifts to satisfy them.
- *Upalalana*: calling meetings and speaking sweet, thoughtful words in order to satisfy the people.
- *Anusasana*: giving instructions on how to become good citizens.

Another example of a divine monarch's nature is found in the *Bhagavatam*'s Fourth Canto. Here, we see that Dhruva left his kingdom to his younger son. Normally, the oldest boy would inherit the throne, but in Dhruva's case, his eldest son, Utakla, was a highly evolved being, free from both material designations and the desire for power. Therefore, he practiced *jada-yoga*, acting as if he were deaf, dumb and imbecilic, so that he would not be given the responsibility of the throne. In this way, he avoided being disturbed by those wishing to sway him from the spiritual path. It is explained in the commentary on this section that the elderly family members and ministers thus assessed Dhruva's two sons and decided that the younger son, Vatasala, should succeed his father.

We know from ancient scriptures that a divine king always consulted the sages and his ministers. The sages or *brahmanas* were responsible for offering unbiased, nonpartisan advice. Divine monarchs were duty bound to follow such advice, because ultimately, divine monarchy was meant to be a sacred rule. The *brahmanas*, who spent their time in spiritual contemplation, could often see beyond the swirling waters of politics to more essential principles—principles that go beyond material conceptions. They were the carriers of spiritual tradition, and were prominent in a time when those who were most enlightened were actually the people responsible for the needs of the entire society. Today, we see quite a different model. Humanity has changed the system so that the masters of coercion and manipulation become leaders. People today are more prone to use the power of personality than the power of soul infusion.

ALTERNATIVE GOVERNMENTS FOR THE CURRENT AGE

As we look at contemporary institutions, both secular and spiritual—particularly in light of a divine monarchy—we wonder what changes could be made in our leadership structure to make society more functional. Given that there are no longer any divine monarchs, can we say that democracy really provides the common ground by which people can choose their rulers? Are there alternatives to democracy?

One alternative is a "rotating" monarchy. Some spiritual and secular groups may be more comfortable with a leader who has monarch-like power within their organization, but who maintains such a position only temporarily. In this scenario, a leader is elected and serves his term.

Another alternative would be to have the responsibilities of the leadership job clearly defined. Then a leader could be given more power than in the average democratic position, but would be able to maintain that power only if he fulfilled the necessary requirements. These requirements would be presented by a nonpartisan board of elders, trustees, etc.

Oligarchy is another option. An oligarchy is a group of "semi-monarchs," or the established elite, who choose a monarch or an executive board from among their own group to serve for a set period of time. That monarch and group function under clearly defined guidelines. The oligarchic group would determine the length of the ruler's term.

The reason that these alternatives would be better than a typical democracy is that these models respect sacred hierarchy. Of course, they only work if the leader is trained and works as a servant-leader, endowed with the ten servant-leadership qualities we have previously discussed. Such people are more likely to allow those who possess more wisdom to lead.

Modern-day organizations, both secular and spiritual, lack real leaders. Real leaders cannot be tied down to board meetings where they are forced to make decisions that best pave the way toward their reelection or where partisan interests overly influence them. These alternative systems, however, give a leader the genuine power to see that the citizens are being cared for.

The highest aspect of spiritual or material management is not possible without drawing in some way on the managerial style of a divine monarch. As a leader comes closer to becoming a divine monarch, he not only has more power but more ability to empower, enliven, protect and care for others. The closer a leader comes to becoming a divine monarch—a true servant-leader—the more we will see the four "C"s—character, competence, compassion, and courage—manifest in his personality. We would see this leader continually discovering truth and presenting values based on that truth.

If, however, servant-leaders cannot be created, then some will say that democracy is perhaps the best system, for they feel that at least in a democracy, the people can feel responsible for their collective successes or failures. However, that conclusion is questionable.

Some say the oligarchic system of shared and monitored monarchy is dangerous, for oligarchies can become poisoned by the desire for power, both individually and collectively. We have all heard the maxim, "Power corrupts, and absolute power corrupts absolutely." So there is always a chance that by increasing a leader's power, we are also increasing the chance that he will become corrupt. This obviously will happen unless the servant-leader sees himself as a steward. He must see that power has come to him to be the caretaker and not the owner. We also know there can be flaws in those who monitor him, for there must always be systems to help monitors, reminding the servant-leader of his responsibilities. Such a monitoring board can be composed of elders, trustees, scholars and saints, with the major influence coming from the guidance and monitoring of detached religious leaders who are spiritual consultants and who understand the genuine needs of the citizens.

In a healthy family, the management of the household is accomplished by the shared power of the mother and father, who often have distinct roles of dominance and control over the children and the various family issues. Although this is a natural and workable arrangement, it can still be abused. In such a situation, there are also various monitors and advisors—elders, community leaders, social workers, the legal system, etc., meant to help the family leaders, and, if necessary, bring them back in line.

All systems are deficient in different ways, but some are more problematic than others. This is the duality inherent in human nature. We are prone to become illusioned and make mistakes; we have imperfect senses and the propensity to cheat others. Although these qualities exist, we still need to coordinate, facilitate and manage our lives. We need leaders.

The main question is: Despite what can and does go wrong, how can we minimize the difficulties and maximize the chances to bring about the highest good for the greatest number of people?

PROTECTION FROM THIEVES AND CHEATERS

Q: In *Srimad-Bhagavatam*, 4.13.20, it is mentioned that where there is no king, thieves flourish. In his purport, Prabhupada mentions that thieves and cheaters are prominent all over the world, and that the government takes no strong action to curb them. Outside of the danger to one's life and property in the presence of thieves and cheaters, how does their presence attack honest people's sense of morality?

A: Not only are there a great number of thieves and rogues among the people, there are thieves and rogues among government officials. Sometimes even the Heads of State function more as rogues than as caretakers of the people. It is the king's duty to create an environment that encourages everyone within his kingdom to strive toward self-realization and love of God. All policies should facilitate this effort. Part of directing that effort is the creation of a strong environment in which qualities such as selflessness, teamwork and, most importantly, the culture of love and trust, are prominent. Thieves and rogues make direct assaults on the culture of love and trust. If contemporary leaders do not effectively deal with the cheating and exploiting mentality, which can be found in all sectors of society, the citizens' ability to take advantage of what this human life is really all about will be minimized.

Providing protection for his subjects is one of the foremost duties of a divine monarch. As such, it is one of the foremost duties of any servant-leader. As mentioned earlier, when people feel cared for and empowered, they tend to be much more effective in all areas of life. When they are not feeling cared for and empowered, they tend to not be effective. Rather, we get what is called in economics "the law of diminishing returns." Without the loving protection of a servant-leader, systems and individuals may be stocked with resources, but the return will be mediocre or minimal.

When an environment is filled with love, compassion and selflessness, and the people's value system is based on hard work, dignity and integrity, productivity will be high. These qualities are contagious. When other citizens enter such an environment, they will automatically be positively influenced. The converse is also true: When an environment is based on posturing, manipulation and exploitation, newcomers will not only be influenced by the atmosphere but will tend to enhance it with their own negative energies.

It is a serious problem for any institution or community when thieves and rogues assault the lives and properties of the proper citizens. However, worse still is when the leader does not effectively deal with such cheaters. Failure to stop thieves and rogues will cause their numbers to increase, and sooner or later the society will descend to a cheating culture. Righteousness and piety will then be lost. Over time, the people will lose sight of standard, proper behavior. That is, society's collective morality will come under attack. When people live in an environment of fear, all their relationships are weakened.

The ancient Vedic scriptures give an example that the sign of a righteous and powerful government is that a woman can dress in fine cloth and gold ornaments, and can sleep under a tree without fear of being harassed or abused. If we take this example as a barometer, we see that practically all regions of the world will fall short. Not only would women be in fear of their safety, this fear would be justified. We can see from this example how powerful the divine monarchs were. Under their rule, citizens were afraid not only to steal but to abuse any other citizen—even when an opportunity seemed to present itself. We should remind ourselves that in the past as well as in the present, leaders who cannot protect their dependents will rarely have strong or serious followers. It is natural for people to seek out a life for themselves in an environment that is secure and where they can feel protected.

Many modern-day corporations create an insecure atmosphere. They use their employees for production and do not care for them in any human way. Employees often find themselves suddenly without jobs as their companies downsize or reconstruct. Of course, when employees are not cared for, they lose their sense of loyalty. They understand that they are not protected because their leaders do not value them. Keeping talent loyal to a corporation has become one of the greatest difficulties faced by many top companies in the Western world. It is a serious issue among Fortune 500 companies in the U.S., especially in the information age.

There are currently many millionaires in America who are under thirty. They are sharp, aggressive, and have much to offer, particularly in the computer industry. But they tend to have few loyalties. They have been trained by their experience to understand that the corporations for which they have been working have little true regard for them. Often, such talented workers leave their corporations for the competition. Now, CEOs are trying to find ways to train and keep the talent that has been recruited by their companies. They are trying to find ways to protect their employees' interests as well as to allow room for creativity, self-esteem and the development of trust in the corporation's vision.

What's in it for the leader who practices servant-leadership? The *Srimad-Bhagavatam*, 4.14.17 states:

> *When the king protects the citizens from disturbances of mischievous ministers, as well as from thieves and rogues, he can, by virtue of such pious activities accept taxes given by his subjects. Thus a pious king can certainly enjoy himself as well as in the life after death.*

The commentary gives a further explanation:

> *The duty of the pious king is described very nicely in this verse. His first and foremost duty is to give protection to the citizens from thieves and rogues as well as from ministers who are no better than thieves and rogues. Formerly, ministers were appointed by the king and were not elected. Consequently, if the king was not very pious or strict, the ministers would become thieves and rogues and exploit the innocent citizens. It is the king's duty to see that there is no increase of thieves and rogues either in the government secretariat or in the departments of public affairs. If the king cannot give protection to the citizens from thieves and rogues or from the government service then in public affairs, he has no right to exact taxes from them. In other words the king or the government can levy taxes from the citizens only if the king or government is able to give protection to the citizens from thieves and rogues.*[6]

---

6   Swami Prabhupada, *Srimad-Bhagavatam*, 4.14.17 purport

We therefore stress that a leader's major function is to protect his dependents. Only then does he have a right to gather taxes, a portion of which are to be used for the citizens' welfare. The *Ramayana* states that it is sinful for a ruler to exact taxes if he is not properly executing his duties. When a ruler thus inappropriately collects taxes, he or she must be chastised by Yamaraja, the Superintendent of Death.

ACCOUNTABILITY OF A LEADER

In the *Hari-bhakti-vilasa*, 1.70, a medieval manual for Vaisnava behavior, it is stated that a spiritual master is responsible for his disciples' sins, that the husband is responsible for the wife's sins, and that the king is responsible for the faults of his counselors. In each case we see the seriousness of responsibility. A spiritual master must consistently guide his disciples so that they will come to a higher platform; otherwise, he will certainly be held accountable and suffer for their sins. A husband's duty is to protect, guide and care for his wife. If he fails in that duty, his wife's sins fall upon him. Similarly, one who is in a leadership position—anyone dealing with the lives of dependents—is held karmically accountable.

If people could really understand the accountability associated with leadership, most would be reluctant to hold such a position. Although much of modernity is based on people thinking that they are units unto themselves, community means seeing our interdependence. We each have an integral role in the function and success of society. Many people these days are trying to avoid the responsibilities and implications of community without realizing that community is actually a great part of the natural order of things.

When there is a cheating mentality prevalent in the government, that mentality will be passed on to the people. There is a story in the *Vedas* concerning a king and his pious *brahmana* advisor named Bhagavan Pandita. While other ministers tried to make their fortune by exploiting the king, Bhagavan Pandita maintained his brahminical detachment. Therefore, the other ministers hated him; his presence interfered with their ability to manipulate and cheat. For this reason, they conspired to minimize Bhagavan Pandita's influence. Perhaps they should kill him, they thought. In the end, they decided that he must be removed from the king's service as chief advisor, perhaps by having him banished from the kingdom.

In the Vedic system, a king would rule for life unless he became mentally incapacitated. The king, however, appointed ministers and their posts were always temporary—depending on the king's needs. Thus the ministers often feared losing their positions. Aside from the ministers, the king was always advised by *brahmanas* who remained free of official position, who were not materialistic, and who were never engaged in partisan politics.

One day, the ministers had a gatekeeper tell Bhagavan Pandita that the king did not want to see him again and that he was no longer welcome in the kingdom. Because of this, the dutiful Pandita left the kingdom of his own volition. After several days, the king began to ask for him. Some of the plotting ministers constructed a false story, saying he had died of a heart attack. The king was shocked to hear this news. He called in the palace doctor to learn more about Bhagavan Pandita's death. The doctor was also part of the ministers' plot, so he confirmed that the Pandita had died from heart failure.

After this, the king was convinced. He decided to reciprocate in some way with the loyal and sensitive service Bhagavan Pandita had rendered while he was alive. Accordingly, he decided to send a donation to the Pandita's widow. He appointed one of the ministers to deliver the money, but the minister instead took the money and divided it between himself and the other ministers involved in the plot. At that same time, Bhagavan Pandita tried to gain entrance into the palace, but to no avail—the ministers' were quite powerful.

One day while the king was out walking in the city, Bhagavan Pandita took the opportunity to try to meet the king. The guards, of course, were aware that this might happen, so they remained vigilant and did not allow Bhagavan Pandita to get close to the king. Finally, Bhagavan Pandita looked to see what direction the king was walking in. He ran ahead and climbed a tall tree. As the king was about to pass under the tree, Bhagavan Pandita began to shout, "Maharaja! Maharaja! It's me, your old friend, Bhagavan Pandita!" Bhagavan was shouting out so desperately that the king looked up and saw his old friend in the tree.

The king immediately walked toward the tree, but the ministers quickly approached him and said, "Don't go there, Your Highness. It's the ghost of Bhagavan Pandita."

At first the king was bewildered. Then he saw that all his ministers were in agreement. "Yes," he thought, "it is a ghost. My ministers have saved me."

The point of this story is to show how people often accept false theories and innocently become part of a culture of manipulation and lying. When the king does not monitor his citizens sufficiently and does not have a strong system for dealing with social deviation, the kingdom will be overrun by thieves, rogues and cheaters. The common people will not only be attacked and abused by such cheaters, but in time, they themselves will become cheaters. We see this all too often in today's society, for we have become a society of the cheaters and the cheated.

PRINCIPLES AND PRACTICES OF JUSTICE

Q: I feel very disturbed as I think of the constant debate on capital punishment, or the government's willingness to plea-bargain in exchange for testimony. However, in this country, we would consider it barbaric to cut a thief's hands off. How do we wade through our conditioning to accept the *Bhagavatam's* statements on these things? Or are these statements examples of *artha-prada*—literally supportive of the goal, but not true in every circumstance?

A: For the health of every society, it is important that the rules of law are clearly understood. It is also important to have a system by which those who break the law are expediently punished. A good justice system is extremely important to the proper functioning of a society. In a lawless civilization, people can break laws without any deterrence.

Part of legal justice is, of course, the citizens' protection from unjust leaders who may use the law to abuse or punish innocent people, or who inflict inappropriate punishments upon criminals. In modern society, people with good sentiments often feel criminals should be forgiven. This shows that they have good intentions. In ancient times, forgiveness was also important, but it was offered only after criminals were punished and corrected. If someone is guilty of an offense but is simply forgiven, this will only reinforce his deviant habits and will not allow the community to feel protected. It will also send a signal to others that deviant behavior is not as bad as they thought it was, and that one can get away with it.

Given that in ancient culture everything was based on creating the highest good for the greatest number of people, each situation was addressed in such a way that it would help the individual as well as benefit society in general. The principle used in punishment was that punishment should fit the crime. After punishment had been administered, forgiveness was offered. Thus punishment primarily addressed the sin rather than the sinner. However, because it was a person who had sinned, punishment was designed to bring out a sense of penance in the criminal's heart. This would help him develop better character and to avoid falling into such problems again. It also made it clear to society that legal deviation would be strictly punished.

Today, there is quite a bit of plea-bargaining and improper legislation. Judicial and executive arrangements are also duplicitous or not in the best interests of the people. It is difficult to form a clear vision of what is proper or exactly how an offender should be dealt with. Often, those offenders who are most successful in avoiding or minimizing consequences for their offenses are those with lawyers skilled in argument and legal loopholes. Sometimes even those who are known to be guilty are released. Therefore, more and more people are finding fault with the legal system, especially in countries like the United States, which has more litigation than any other country in the world. Americans tend to engage in litigation over the slightest disturbances. Filing and winning lawsuits can be so lucrative that there are even children who sue their own parents, often on ridiculous grounds.

In ancient Vedic times when we had a divine monarch, the legislators, executives, and judicial officials were righteous. They worked for the benefit of society as a whole. If a person with such authority ever became a lawbreaker—a threat to the royal order as well as to the citizens' peace—heavy penalties were imposed.

Today, it is difficult for pious people to condone capital punishment. The divine monarch of ancient times, however, clearly supported it. Of course, under a divine monarch, there was little need to implement such a drastic punishment. Because of the divine love that pervaded the atmosphere, no one would even think of committing a crime punishable by death. Capital punishment is for the most serious crimes, and these were few in Vedic times.

The king understood the spiritual aspects of capital punishment. The law of *karma* dictates that we are materially and spiritually responsible for our actions and will receive a commensurate reaction. The reaction we receive is in keeping with the action we have performed. If we give charity, we will receive charity; if we kill someone, we ourselves will be killed. Often these reactions do not come about in our current life but sit like seeds in our hearts, ready to sprout in the next life. A divine monarch had the power to allow a murderer, for example, to experience his karmic reaction in this life and thus end the cycle of violence with the end of this life. In that sense, capital punishment was seen as an act of mercy.

However, capital punishment should not be implemented in a society that does not have a strong and honest legal system. Instead of punishing serious criminals, innocent people are sometimes accused, tried and convicted. In most cases, the government can no longer tell the difference between the innocent and the guilty. Because of legal manipulation, it is dangerous even to sentence an alleged criminal to life in prison. He may be innocent. In this case, capital punishment would be a travesty of justice.

Another issue often misunderstood is that in some ancient cultures a great king would use excessive punishments when dealing with offenders. The Vedic scriptures mention that a king could chop off a thief's hands, for example. This instruction falls into the category of what Bhaktivinoda Thakura (one of the most prominent spiritual teachers in the Vaisnava line and a high court judge in Bengal in the late 1800s) called the difference between *artha-prada*, instructions meant to support a goal which are themselves not transcendental, and *paramartha-prada*, eternal instructions meant to be followed at all times and in all circumstances. The *artha-prada* instructions usually deal with the phenomenal world and provide information on such things as medicine, music, history, culture and politics. The *paramartha-prada* deals with transcendence, theology and mysticism. *Artha-prada* instructions are subject to human scrutiny and are not absolute; *paramartha-prada* instructions are divine and beyond human reasoning. They are not subject to human scrutiny or adjustment. Ancient Indian scriptures tend to merge these two types of instructions in one place. Therefore, we can understand that many of the explicit instructions relating to how a government functions are not absolute. Rather, when we work with the material energy, we must look at time, place and circumstance to determine the best course of action.

We must also apply the *paramartha* principles to all of our activities while deciding our course of action. When the scriptures present to us *paramartha-prada*, this is also associated with a certain context. So divine monarch is not really a post in which someone can be superficially positioned. Rather, it is most functional when there is a truly divine person. He or she will naturally create divine order. Since such a divine person rarely arises, one may ask, "What is the need for examining this type of government?" As we observe something in its optimum state we get a deeper understanding of certain goals and higher standards that we should try to attain. The closer we get to the actual goal, the more auspicious and successful everything will be. But without understanding the highest goals, we will find ourselves settling with lower and lower standards.

Again, many of the instructions on how to deal with criminals, etc., are not absolute. However, the spirit of the instructions should be understood. That is, unless there is a clear vision about how the criminal element will be deterred, a ruler cannot be said to be protecting his people. A culture of deviation and exploitation will be fostered instead of a culture of trust and righteousness.

If a person is truly interested in spirituality, he or she must constantly remember to avoid dogma and not mistake dry rules and regulations for spirituality. Rather, they should focus on the essence, not the external shell. It is the spirit of divine love—which expresses itself in progressive and ever-expanding ways—that we want to contact and bring into our lives. Those who pursue merely a formal orthodoxy will be viewed as superficial—not getting at the essence of religious truth.

As we observe people participating in modern-day society, we want to create a bridge that many can walk across, allowing them to embrace transcendence. Some of the rules and activities of antiquity are secondary, though they were helpful given the time and atmosphere in which they were originally employed. In some cases, they were part of the *artha-prada*, and so they are subject to scrutiny to see whether or not they are still relevant in the modern context.

Now, people may misuse the principle of *paramartha-prada/artha-prada*, and they often do. An expert *acarya* is able to adjust things according to time, place and circumstance. But this is not easy, because there will be discrepancies where there is not sufficient realization and empowerment. When you think about it, however, what we are really dealing with here is damage control. Not only will we have problems with the leader or leaders, but we will constantly have problems with the advisors or any kind of check and balance system. There will always be room for error, cheating, exploitation, etc. It is only when God, His incarnations or empowered agents rule that we have proper order. Otherwise, we look at the highest model and endeavor to come as close to it as possible. One who exploits this system should be treated like a thief.

The Sufi tradition tells us how to best deal with thieves. Thieves do not like to rob poor homes. Rather, they look for homes where the residents have been successful. So how do we deal with a thief who has broken into our home? It is dangerous to meet him with a weapon; he may have a stronger weapon and we may be killed. Often, the best way to deal with a thief is to simply turn on the light. When the light is turned on, the thief will flee. The real thief in our lives is *maya*, illusion, or what the Christians call "Satan" or the Muslims "Nafs." By turning on the light of purity and devotion, the "*maya* thief" will be defeated. If our rulers continue to maintain personal integrity, ethics, morality and purity, there will be far fewer thieves among them and their subjects, and thus far less need for punishment.

Moreover, punishment itself is not necessarily a solution to the problem of criminality. It does serve as a deterrent, but it does not in itself create an environment in which people are not morally inclined to commit crime. A servant-leader will want to create such an environment. In some third-world countries such as parts of Africa, India and in some Muslim countries, when a thief is caught in a marketplace or village, he is often beaten to death as a form of instant justice. We find, however, that this severe punishment does not really deter crime. There is still much thievery in these countries. Expedient and hard justice may be necessary sometimes, but it does not seem to be the real factor in bringing about peace within society.

CRIMINAL JUSTICE IN MODERN SUPERPOWERS

During my recent travels in Africa, Argentina, Mexico, Bosnia, Russia and the United States, I met with penal officials and addressed the media on crime. I have also conducted seminars on issues of justice and servant-leadership. In these discussions, I often ask people what they consider the most amazing and unfortunate things that Russia, the United States and South Africa have in common. People tend to list a number of commonalities, but rarely do they realize that the one thing they have most in common is that these three countries have more of their citizens in prison than any other countries. The United States has the most, then South Africa, then Russia. Incarceration of citizens is increasing so much in the United States that it is turning into a profitable business. In the late 1990s, it cost taxpayers about thirty-five thousand dollars to maintain an average prisoner for one year, and about fifty thousand dollars for every new cell built. Incarcerating people is an expensive affair. Many U.S. citizens can live comfortably on thirty-five thousand dollars per year, but to support the criminals, their salaries are being taxed so that their take-home pay is much less.

The most recent statistics about imprisonment in the U.S. are astounding! If the present rate of incarceration continues over the next fifty years, almost half of the American population will be in jail. Even though so many people are going to jail, the U.S. still has the highest homicide rate of any Western country. Fifty percent of all illicit drugs being used in the international arena find their market in the U.S.

The U.S. is by far the most violent industrialized nation in the world. One-third of all Americans own a handgun. Thousands of weapons are brought into the school system every day by students. Here we can see that although the U.S. has such a developed prison system, it has not solved its crime problem. Obviously, this has a lot to do with improper crime prevention. Crime prevention is not just a matter of legislation but of creating an atmosphere that genuinely deters offenders. Such an atmosphere must emphasize the higher principles of life.

It is interesting, too, to note what the American people think about themselves: Seventy percent of them believe that there are no real leaders in this country. As strong leadership is lost, the citizens' deviations will naturally increase.

WHEN THE KING MAKES MISTAKES

Q: In *Bhagavatam*, 4.13.23, both verse and purport discuss the importance of tolerating the king's behavior even when he is wrong, because the king is the representative of God (*nara-narayana*). My first thought in reading this was that this particular conversation in the *Bhagavatam* is happening between Vidura and Maitreya. Vidura is surprised that the sages would curse and kill a king. Although Vidura is technically a *sudra* due to his mother's being a maidservant, he is the son of Vyasadeva and is the incarnation of Yamaraja. His sense of *dharma* is very strong. He is also a pure devotee of Krishna. Therefore, more than anyone, he is qualified to appreciate just how terrible Vena's sin must have been for the sages to have intervened and killed him.

A: In the story about the killing of King Vena, we see that the sages were particularly concerned that the previous king's absence would allow rogues and thieves to torment the citizens. They realized that they needed to install a king as soon as possible. This is why they encouraged Vena to ascend the throne in the first place. His father had renounced the throne and left for the forest to perform meditation. The sages recognized Vena's cruel nature, but he was the king's son. It is interesting to note here that while the sages wanted Vena to ascend the throne, the ministers were against it. Vena was cruel and wicked by nature. The ministers could never support such a king. The sages, however, seem to have had more influence on the decision, and Vena was enthroned. This contrasts with the example set by King Uttanapada in choosing his son, Dhruva, to rule after him. Uttanapada consulted the ministers, the *brahmanas* and the citizens, then studied Dhruva's qualities himself to ensure that he would be succeeded by a worthwhile son. In Vena's case, Vena's father had already left the palace and no one could find him. The ministers did not agree with the sages, and the kingdom was filled with inauspiciousness because of this.

Later, the sages heard of the people's suffering and decided to meet with Vena. They warned him that he would be in danger if he continued in his cruelty toward others and in his insistence that worship be stopped in his empire. When he refused to heed them, even blaspheming the Supreme Lord, the sages realized that he must be dethroned if the citizens were to be protected. Vena dealt strictly with criminals, but still his government was poor, being based on principles of cruelty and atheism rather than on goodness and God consciousness. In the end, the *brahmanas* chanted *mantras* with the power to kill Vena, and he was thus successfully removed from the throne.

The king is supposed to be the representative of God in human form (*naradeva*, or *nara-narayana*). Therefore, the *Srimad-Bhagavatam* tells us to tolerate the king's acts, even if they appear to be wrong. In *Srimad-Bhagavatam*, 4.13.23, it says:

> *It is the duty of all citizens in the state never to insult the king, even though he sometimes appears to have done something very sinful. Because of his prowess, the king is always more influential than all other ruling chiefs.*

The keywords here are "insult" and "appears." In most ancient cultures, people were reluctant to insult the monarch, because as God's representative, he was in a powerful position and was supposed to have divine insight into how to benefit the citizens. The monarch was therefore given much freedom, tolerance and support. If a monarch made a mistake, the citizens were expected to tolerate it.

Now, when we apply this tolerance to modern culture, to communities and to institutions and corporations, we can see the value of tolerating a leader's mistakes as long as the leader has his dependents' well-being in mind. That is, we can tolerate a leader's honest mistakes if his motives are correct. This does not mean that we should deny the mistake, but we can help the leader learn from the mistake. Otherwise, we can use the leader's mistake to cloud our relationship with him and to take away his influence. It is different when the dependents feel that the mistake was not so honest, or that the leader does not have their best interests in mind. In modern society, leaders make many mistakes. This is not such a problem. The real problem is when a leader makes a mistake and tries to cover it up, or when the mistake is part of a general sort of deviance, lack of integrity, lack of ethics or morality, or is done secretively. Such leaders obviously do not have the highest interest in their dependents.

When a leader tries to act as if he is free of mistakes, it is worse than if he merely makes mistakes. This is so because it reveals his arrogance and lack of honesty, which will cause his dependents to lose faith in him.

The worst, however, is when a mistake is made by a leader, denied or not denied, and it is based on self-centered interest rather than on the interests of his constituents' welfare. When there is proper servant-leadership, then mistakes can be fixed because of the servant-leader's honesty. His constituents can help him face the crisis caused by his mistake and, together, they can correct it.

Great leaders know that mistakes and failures are simply opportunities to understand what is necessary to become successful. Thomas Edison made over a thousand errors in his pursuit of developing the light bulb. Rather than becoming discouraged, he saw each mistake as bringing him closer to success. In that sense, mistakes are not mistakes. In any case, the verse emphasizes that we should not be overly disturbed if we see that our leader makes a mistake.

The other key word in this verse is "insult." When people lack culture, they tend to overreact. If a leader has made a mistake, a reaction is natural. But to go so far as to insult a good person for his mistake is an overreaction. That people insult their leaders over mistakes is also a sign that they do not see their connection with the leader or with the issue over which the mistake was committed. Servant-leaders should therefore build teamship. Building a team means building a culture of trust. Then, if there is a mistake (or even an apparent mistake), they will want to help solve the problem it creates rather than denigrate the person who committed it. In a culture of envy, people hope their leaders will make mistakes so that they can tear them down in an attempt to regain their so-called independence.

Later, the same *Bhagavatam* text mentions that Vena was cursed because his sinful activities were grievous. This indicates that Vena did not have good intentions toward his citizens. Rather, he was a self-centered leader—abusive and exploitative. Therefore, the sages took it upon themselves to try to first rectify him, and when that didn't seem to work, they resolved to remove him, to bring about his demise.

And how did they take his life? They simply chanted *mantras*. The sages had such power and purity that simply by chanting *mantras*, they were able to force his soul out of his physical body. This is Vedic culture: The king has great power, but the sages have greater power based on their purity, their performance of austerity and their knowledge of scripture. Therefore, it was their duty to monitor the king and to be sure he always practiced stewardship toward the people.

THE CITIZENS MUST PERFORM THEIR DUTIES

Q: There is also the example of Yudhisthira. When Yudhisthira saw how well Duryodhana was ruling, he decided not to demand back his kingdom but to request only five villages, one for each of the Pandava brothers. "As *ksatriyas*, the only proper livelihood of the Pandavas was to rule, and not to accept any other occupation." Duryodhana refused with his famous line, "No, sir. What to speak of five villages, we cannot spare even so much land which can hold the point of a needle."

Duryodhana's sin here, which is said to have contributed to his downfall and lead up to the Kuruksetra War, was the same as Vena's sin: the king did not allow the citizens, or a section of the citizens, to perform their ordinary duties.[7]

It is the king's duty to ensure that people follow their duty in the *varnasrama* system, which would gradually elevate them to the spiritual plane. The *varnasrama* system is designed to create interdependence and therefore cooperation in society. It is also designed to keep social balance in a world where various people are affected by different combinations of the modes.

Can you speak about the importance of social interdependence and why it is so important to maintain it?

A: It is interesting that the sin Duryodhana committed and which led up to the Kuruksetra war was similar to the sin Vena committed. That is, they did not allow the citizens (or a section of the citizens) to perform their prescribed duties. To allow the citizens to perform their prescribed duties is one of the prime duties of the divine monarch. Thus, a divine monarch ensures that his people are properly engaged, taking into consideration their natural propensities. As we mentioned earlier, one who is properly engaged according to his or her designation in the *varnasrama* system can be satisfied. It is the king's duty to help his subjects seek such personal and social satisfaction. When the king does not engage the citizens properly, but allows them to engage

---

7   Swami Prabhupada, *Srimad-Bhagavatam*, 4.14.9

in whimsical or sinful activities, chaos is the result. In today's society we can see that allowing citizens to indulge their whims has led to the creation of slaughterhouses, organized gambling, legalized prostitution, drug abuse, etc. Leaders who allow or encourage such things are responsible for one-sixth of the sins committed by their citizens. The king also receives one-fourth of his citizens' pious credits.

Thus there is interdependence between the leader and the constituents and also among the citizens. That interdependence also spreads into the relationship between the people and the moving and nonmoving species of life. Everything and everyone is part of an ecosystem. We are all affected by the actions of everyone else.

The *varnasrama* system is designed to facilitate this interdependence. When the persons in one *varna* or *ashrama* follow their prescribed duty properly, the other *varnas* and *ashramas* are automatically encouraged to do the same in order to keep balance. When the mercantile class is properly producing food and engaging in business, the society's "breadbasket" is maintained. The merchants are taxed by the king, who should also be behaving according to his prescribed duty of giving charity to the *brahmanas* (intellectuals and priests) and the poor. The *brahmanas* can then concentrate on their duty of cultivating knowledge of matter and spirit.

The converse is also true. If one class is dysfunctional, other classes will not be able to properly engage in their prescribed duties and there will be social imbalance.

PROMOTING INTERDEPENDENCE

Varnasrama-dharma is based on honoring the diversity in unity that is the natural consequence of interdependence. When there is forced conformity, there will never be true unity; when there is simply diversity without any attempt at unity, this is anarchy. The divine monarch's duty is to expertly engage the people according to their individual natures and responsibilities toward the central goal of developing a balanced society.

A divine monarch seeks to synergize his kingdom. Synergy literally means that the total effect is greater than the sum of the individual elements. One plus one equals more than two. The ability to synergize a kingdom comes from celebrating the diversity among one's subjects and then holding them accountable to fulfill both personal and social goals. It does not result from either dependent or independent citizens, but from those who recognize their interdependence.

Recognizing interdependence also results in the formation of symbiotic relationships. That is, relationships based on mutual need. In a symbiotic relationship, what it takes to maintain two distinct living entities is actually reduced as the two entities support each other's needs and help one another attain success. When the king honors unity in diversity, it allows for symbiotic relationships among his subjects wherein all benefit.

For interdependence to work, however, there has to be a common ground upon which the diversity expresses itself.

Without that common ground or common goal, society will fall into chaos.

Diversity experts realize that by celebrating diversity, we can avoid four "cancers" that are detrimental to the achievement of synergy. These are:

- Criticism
- Complaint
- Comparison
- Competition

Without celebrating diversity, we may exist, but will we flourish? In such a condition, we will not optimize our potential. Unless we learn to cooperate, we will only compromise. We must do away with divisive factors if we are to achieve synergy.

Too much independence destabilizes an institution or community because it produces anarchy. When there is social fragmentation, people will not bring out their best. Also, too much dependence is unhealthy because people will not be creative. They will not use their own initiative in performing their tasks but will tend to be dull and uninvolved on a personal level.

Nowadays, people are discussing codependency, which manifests at its worst in addictive behaviors. Codependency is often at conflict with one's God consciousness, because the codependent person replaces God with his or her spouse, child, business or a substance such as alcohol or cocaine. Every form of addiction is a misdirected religion. John Bradshaw, in his best-selling book, *Healing the Shame that Binds You*, discusses some of the dangers of addiction. He stresses how every addiction is an aborted religion—how it has a God, disciplines, devotees and rituals. The rituals might be seen in the way one passes around a marijuana joint, for example, or the way in which one drinks alcohol with friends.

Addictions have their moment of ecstasy, and their atonement. All addicts and codependent people are spiritually bankrupt. They are actually searching after the ecstasy that comes from God, but they look in all the wrong places. Bradshaw explains how shame is necessary for recovery, and that in codependency and addiction, one is overreacting to things outside and underreacting to things inside. Addicts believe something outside will bring them happiness. In materialistic society, where addiction is rampant, people tend to want to look for their happiness outside themselves rather than finding it within. A divine monarch helps people to focus more on both their individuality and their interdependence, and he himself leads from the inside out. His leadership example stimulates them to also look for inner happiness.

WHERE DOES A LEADER'S RESPONSIBILITY BEGIN AND END?

Q: In *Srimad-Bhagavatam*, 4.13.37, King Anga is described in Sanskrit as *udara-dhi*, which translates as "liberal-minded." The full definition of the word actually provides a list of qualities suitable to a king: "high, lofty, exalted, great, best, noble, illustrious, generous, upright, honest, liberal, gentle, munificent, sincere, proper, right, eloquent, unperplexed, highly intelligent and wise." The use of this particular word also gives us an insight into King Anga's character. The commentators say:

> "*Udara-dhi* means one who has a broader outlook... The meaning of the word *udara-dhi* is *buddhiman*—intelligent or considerate. Because of this, even for one's own sense gratification one engages in the devotional service of Lord Krishna."
>
> ***Caitanya-caritamrta,***
> ***- Madhya-lila, 24.91***

Anga was advised by the *brahmanas* to ask the Lord for a son. Prabhupada writes in his purport:

> *Since the King was very liberal, the Supreme Personality of Godhead, in order to increase his detachment from this material world, willed that a cruel son be born of the Queen so that the King would have to leave home. As stated above, Lord Vishnu fulfills the desires of the karmis as they desire, but the Lord fulfills the desire of a devotee in a different way so that the devotee may gradually come to Him.*[8]

Later, Anga leaves home. In doing so, he knowingly abandoned his citizens, who were like his children, to Vena's cruelty and irreligiosity. So although we are speaking of leadership and the responsibility and duty of maintaining the people, here is an example of a king who abandoned his duty both because he felt he had failed to protect the citizens from his son (the *Bhagavatam* tells us he tried to rectify Vena in various ways but failed) and to answer the higher calling of spiritual life. Where, therefore, does a ruler's responsibility begin and end?

A: Those who are surrendered to the Lord are more directly under the Lord's care. The Supreme Lord will arrange things to benefit our growth. Sometimes these things come in unusual ways. Sometimes they appear as difficulties. In this case, Anga was given a cruel son to help him focus more on his ultimate goal of self-realization.

Let me try to address the question of a leader's responsibility—where does it begin and end? One in a

---

[8] Swami Prabhupada, *Srimad-Bhagavatam*, 4.13.37 purport

leadership position must always be responsible. There should never come a time when a leader is not responsible. A leader should have integrity both in his personal and public lives. A leader should also be conscious that whatever he does, others will follow his example.

Therefore, accepting the position of leader means accepting the constant awareness that whatever we do is always both under scrutiny and is subject to being followed. A leader must always be aware of the effect his actions have on others, especially those whom he is representing. For a leader to decide whether or not to leave his position should be based on what would be best for both the present and future. It's common in today's society for leaders to remain in their positions long after they have become irrelevant or incompetent simply because they wish to continue to enjoy the perks that come from having the position. Servant-leaders know when they are no longer the best person to facilitate particular situations. Since servant-leaders haven't necessarily wanted power but accepted it so as to facilitate others, they will eagerly step down when someone else can better facilitate the caring process.

In leadership, we should always be honest about our shortcomings. Even if we have made mistakes, we should always maintain the interests of our dependents. Part of honesty is knowing when to step down—when we see we are no longer benefiting others by our leadership. If we are able to be this honest, our honesty and our legacy will be respected.

DIFFICULTIES FROM FAMILY

> *Vidura inquired from the sage Maitreya: My dear brahmana, King Anga is very gentle. He had a high character and was a saintly personality and lover of brahminical culture. How is it that such a great soul got a bad son like Vena, because of whom he became indifferent to his kingdom and left it?*
>
> -*Srimad-Bhagavatam*, 4.13.21

From Srila Prabhupada's purport:

> *In family life a man is supposed to live happily with father, mother, wife and children, but sometimes, under certain conditions, a father, mother, child or wife becomes an enemy. It is said by Canakya Pandita, a great political consult from India, that a father is an enemy when he is too much in debt, a mother is an enemy if she marries for a second time, a wife is an enemy when she is very beautiful, and a son is an enemy when he is a foolish rascal. In this way, when a family member becomes an enemy it is a very difficult to live in family life or remain a householder...*

Here we see that there are certain difficulties that one may face in family life. These are definitely controversial. Vena was, however, a cruel and foolish son. He was Anga's enemy.

Unable to rectify him, his father neither accepted his son nor turned a blind eye to his deviations. Instead, he chose to follow the higher calling of spiritual life and to leave home for a life of renunciation and meditation. Here we see that when a servant-leader makes a decision, it must be based on what is best for the present as well as the future. Obviously, he has to prioritize. When that decision is based on the higher calling of pursuing one's spiritual life, then that takes precedence over everything else.

WHEN LEADERS QUIT THEIR POSTS

Q: When thinking of leadership in most institutions, is it possible to judge those who appear to be abandoning responsibility for similar reasons? In Anga's case, we know that the Lord desired him to leave home and therefore arranged an adverse situation to drive him out. Unfortunately, we rarely have such direct evidence about other people's choices. What attitude should we take toward those who disappoint their followers by leaving their leadership posts to pursue their spiritual lives? Can we assume that the Lord is working with all who are sincere and that they are obeying His directives, even if they choose paths different than what was expected of them?

A: Often people resign, run away or change services due to the difficulties of the work. They become discouraged, frustrated or just lose their desire to maintain their responsibilities. However, sometimes they feel changing services will give them more responsibilities, and they want this. They want more of a challenge. Whenever our leaders give up one service for another, it is not always easy for us to judge their motivations. This is especially true of those on the spiritual path. Such persons may be receiving inspiration from the Lord. It is best to leave the judgment of their behavior up to God.

> *One cannot avoid the order of the Supreme Personality of Godhead, not by the strength of severe austerities, an exalted Vedic education, or the power of mystic yoga, physical prowess or intellectual activities. Nor can one use his power of religion, his material opulence or any other means, either by himself or with the help of others, to defy the orders of the Supreme Lord. That is not possible for any living being, from Brahma down to the ant.*
>
> **-Srimad-Bhagavatam, 5.1.12**

If we look at great prophets, *acaryas*, and even some great thinkers in the ordinary sense of the word, we will see that the decisions they make to pursue their callings are often quite abrupt. Part of their greatness is that they were absolutely willing to answer their calling when it came. We can also look at the lives of Zoraster, Moses, Abdu'l-Baha, Jesus, Muhammad, Buddha, Ramanujacarya, Madhvacarya,

Sankaracarya, Nimbarakacarya, Lord Caitanya, and so on, and see that all of them led quite revolutionary lives. They left the orthodoxy or accepted courses of action to answer something higher that was coming from within them. One cannot avoid the Lord's order. If we try to avoid it, we will never be satisfied.

WHEN LEADERS ARE TOO NICE

Q: Lord Vishnu used Anga's good qualities to bring him pain. The verse says that Anga was liberal-minded, and therefore he gave a portion of the sweet drink to his wife, although she was unqualified. It was obvious that Anga's action would cause distress not only to himself but to his citizens as well, because what affects the king (or the father) affects his subordinates. What ultimate responsibility does a leader hold for the pain he causes others by his misjudgment of a situation, or simply his "liberal-mindedness?" Is it dependent on his motive? Where does God's protection come in, both for the citizens and for the leader? How should a leader feel if his attempt to perform a good action leads his followers into trouble?

A: A divine monarch or true leader always sees himself as responsible for mistakes that hurt his dependents. Therefore, a leader is always careful to evaluate a planned course of action before embarking on it. Because a leader is trained to feel mercy toward the citizens as well as to be cautious in his behavior, he is less likely to at times appear incompetent or foolish in his management. When he does not know the best course of action, he consults the competent people with whom he has surrounded himself. In the event that a mistake is committed, however, a leader will apologize and try to rectify the damage. He will not deny his mistake or pass the responsibility for it off on others.

God's mercy is always available. There is never a time when the Lord's mercy is unavailable, and there is never a time when even the most inauspicious situation cannot be turned into an educational and productive experience.

Teachers are very important, of course, and as a leader, if he or she is divinely inspired and has good intentions, this will minimize failures and embarrassments. Such a leader who accepts good counsel, divine care and blessings will be cared for and well guided. Therefore, he will be able to care for and guide others. Such a leader knows the consequences of improper guidance or the abuse of that with which he has been endowed. He will know the serious consequences of his own deviation. Like a parent who finds that his or her actions have put their children into difficulty, he or she will quickly try to rectify the situation. The divine monarch or a powerful servant-leader cares for his dependents as much as a mother cares for her children, knowing them as well as a mother knows her offspring. Such knowledge and care will constantly bring auspiciousness for the dependents as well as for the leader, and there will be a constant exchange of appreciation and affection that will empower them both.

THE POWER OF AUSTERITY

Q: An interesting point about Vena is that he received the throne by default when his father left. He had refused his father's good training, and he is one of the few rulers mentioned in the *Bhagavatam* who did not perform austerities before ascending the throne. He did not recognize a higher power. Rather, he usurped the Lord's position, calling himself the Supreme Personality of Godhead and calling the sages who insisted that Lord Vishnu be worshiped "unchaste," as if they were giving up their husband to search after some paramour to worship.[9] Even great demons mentioned in the Vedic literature, like Ravana and Kamsa, recognized a superior power and performed austerities to receive their power. So Vena is somewhat special in this regard. It is mentioned that from the austerities performed by a prospective king, he attains all eight mystic opulences, which help him in ruling his kingdom.[10]

Why is it important for a prospective king to undergo austerities? Besides mystic powers, what does he gain from it?

A: Austerities are known as *tapasya*. These austerities can just as easily be performed for material benefit as for spiritual benefit. When they are performed to enhance one's spiritual life or the attainment of God consciousness, they are called *tapo-divyam*. Austerity helps us focus on our goals, whatever they are. Materially speaking, the performance of austerity helps a person develop both hard and soft skills that can help them in their leadership. By "hard" and "soft" skills,

9   Swami Prabhupada, *Srimad-Bhagavatam*, 4.14.23
10 Swami Prabhupada, *Srimad-Bhagavatam*, 4.14.4

I am referring to physical technique (hard) and relationship and communication issues (soft). The performance of *tapo-divyam* enhances our natural strengths, allows us to become more empathetic, builds our enthusiasm and increases our detachment. Austerity performed for a material goal brings lesser but similar results, although not usually detachment.

Problems with a leader often have more to do with mental attachments and weaknesses within the leader than anything else. The performance of austerity can help a leader gain perspective and become less enamored with his own mind. It can also help a leader develop enough detachment that true integrity becomes possible.

The performance of austerity is most essential for those wishing to develop self-control and to build their character. There are different types of austerities: austerities of the mind, words and actions. Just as one can be offensive to others in his thoughts, words or actions, so one can facilitate others in his thoughts, words and actions.

Austerities of the mind include thinking assertively, positively, compassionately and not allowing the mind to be captured by lust but to focus it on loving and caring for others. The *Bhagavad-gita*, 17.16 states:

> *And satisfaction, simplicity, gravity, self-control and purification of one's existence are the austerities of the mind.*

A.C. Bhaktivedanta Swami Prabhupada's purport states:

To make the mind austere is to detach it from sense gratification. It should be so trained that it can be always thinking of doing good for others. The best training for the mind is gravity in thought. One should not deviate from God consciousness and must always avoid sense gratification. To purify one's nature is to become God conscious. Satisfaction of the mind can be obtained only by taking the mind away from thoughts of sense enjoyment. The more we think of sense enjoyment, the more the mind becomes dissatisfied. In the present age we unnecessarily engage the mind in so many different ways for sense gratification, and so there is no possibility of the mind's becoming satisfied. The best course is to divert the mind to the Vedic literature, which is full of satisfying stories, as in the Puranas and the Mahabharata. One can take advantage of this knowledge and thus become purified. The mind should be devoid of duplicity, and one should think of the welfare of all. Silence means that one is always thinking of self-realization. The person in God consciousness observes perfect silence in this sense. Control of the mind means detaching the mind from sense enjoyment. One should be straightforward in his dealings and thereby purify his existence. All these qualities together constitute austerity in mental activities.

Austerity of speech means speaking truth in a palatable way:

> *Austerity of speech consists in speaking words that are truthful, pleasing, beneficial, and not agitating to others, and also in regularly reciting Vedic literature.*
>
> **-Bhagavad-gita, 17.15**

One should not speak in such a way as to agitate the minds of others. Of course, when a teacher speaks, he can speak the truth for the instruction of his students, but such a teacher should not speak to those who are not his students if he will agitate their minds. This is penance as far as talking is concerned. Besides that, one should not talk nonsense. The process of speaking in spiritual circles is to say something upheld by the scriptures. One should at once quote from scriptural authority to back up what he is saying. At the same time, such talk should be very pleasurable to the ear. By such discussions, one may derive the highest benefit and elevate human society. There is a limitless stock of Vedic literature, and one should study this. This is called penance of speech.[11]

Austerity of action refers to engaging in those activities that will enhance one's ability to control his senses and allow him to use them in such a way as to help his environment.

---

11   Swami Prabhupada, *Bhagavad gita*, 17.15 purport

> *Austerity of the body consists in worship of the Supreme Lord, the brahmanas, the spiritual master, and superiors like the father and mother, and in cleanliness, simplicity, celibacy and nonviolence.*
>
> *-Bhagavad-gita,* 17.14

One should offer, or learn to offer, respect to God or to the demigods, the perfect, qualified brahmanas and the spiritual master and superiors like father, mother or any person who is conversant with Vedic knowledge. These should be given proper respect. One should practice cleansing oneself externally and internally, and he should learn to become simple in behavior. He should not do anything which is not sanctioned by the scriptural injunctions. He should not indulge in sex outside of married life, for sex is sanctioned in the scripture only in marriage, not otherwise. This is called celibacy. These are penances and austerities as far as the body is concerned.[12]

So often we have seen how people have acquired a position or received an opportunity freely, without having undergone any austerity to obtain it. Such people often take their position for granted. When a person is born in a rich family, he does not have to endeavor for much, even in childhood. These children often become resentful of the opportunities they have been given. On the other hand, a child who has been born in a poor

---
12   Swami Prabhupada, *Bhagavad gita*, 17.14 purport

family and who has had to work for everything he has, will appreciate the value of what he has earned.

BUILDING CHARACTER

Q: Aside from developing mystic opulences, austerity is character-building. What means do our leaders have available to them in these times to build character?

A: Character building is the most important priority in leadership. We can say that compassion and humility are the mothers of virtue, but character, competence and courage are the fathers of virtue, particularly character. With character, one can get what money cannot buy.

- You can buy a bed but not sleep.
- You can buy a book but not brains.
- You can buy clothes but not beauty.
- You can buy medicine but not good health.
- You can buy a house but not a home.
- You can buy people but not friends.
- You can buy a temple but not God.
- You can buy reputation but not character.

The most important things in life are earned by strong character and sacrifice. Externals, like money, are not enough. It takes genuine commitment and a development of higher consciousness. The dictionary defines character as "the aggregate of features or traits that form the individual nature of a person or thing; ... moral or ethical quality; qualities of honesty, fortitude, etc.; integrity."

The crime rate is ever increasing due to moral poverty. One congressman recently told me that we are "slowly becoming a culture that says that the only right thing is to get by, the only wrong thing is to get caught. If it feels good, do it, and if you don't want to do it, don't. If you don't like it anymore, divorce it. If it becomes inconvenient, divorce it. If you can't handle it, drink or drug your problems away." This is true because people have no cohesive sense of morality to guide them in their actions. Therefore, they are left only with their sensual desires.

This is not an era where most people function according to ethics. They have no clear understanding of morality or personal integrity, because they have been taught to live their lives based on relativism. Speculation and relativism can never develop a strong culture of productivity, love and trust. Such a low-trust culture will interfere with teamship and synergy and will constantly produce bad managers and poor leaders.

In *Srimad-Bhagavatam*, 1.1.6, it is said that no one should accept a position of authority over others unless his character is spotless. This is the Age of Kali, or quarrel, and the pillars of this age are illicit sex, animal slaughter, intoxication and gambling. Building character means avoiding these activities and, if possible, protecting others from falling prey to them. The *Bhagavatam* states that a leader must protect and care not only for his constituents, but even for the plant and animal life within his kingdom.

> *The four leaders of the human society, namely the sannyasis, the brahmana, the king and the public leader, must be tested crucially by their character and qualification. Before one can be accepted as a spiritual or material master of society, he must be tested by the above-mentioned criteria of character. Such public leaders may be less qualified in academic qualifications, but it is necessary primarily that they be free from the contamination of the four disqualifications, namely gambling, drinking, prostitution and animal slaughter.[13]*

King Uttanapada tested his son's character. King Pariksit also showed strong character. It was his strength of character, his integrity, that allowed him to rule a vast empire.

We can develop stronger character by studying others who have outstanding character. Character is the ability to rise above self-interest for the sake of others. Character is who you are when others are not watching. For example, we can reinforce our consciousness by allowing what we are in private to be open to public scrutiny. Character is shaped by how we choose our everyday thoughts, words, and actions.

- Watch your thoughts—they become words.
- Watch your words—they become actions.
- Watch your actions—they become habits.
- Watch your habits—they become character.
- Watch your character—it becomes your culture.

---

13   Swami Prabhupada, *Srimad-Bhagavatam*, 1.17.41 purport

This list helps us reflect on how thoughts, words and deeds are integrated into habits that are responsible for our character development. As we are more focused on our thoughts, words and deeds, we will naturally develop better character. Conversely, no one can have good character if he or she is weak in any of these areas. Integrity, after all, means wholeness.

Many people have poor character because they lack courage. They may not have the boldness to stand up against negative opposition and to support truth, service and justice. Therefore, they succumb to deviations.

Another obstacle in building character is when we become caught up in temporary pleasure. We should be careful not to confuse temporary pleasure with enduring happiness. Pleasure is an event; enduring happiness is a process. Pleasure is often something that we attain easily and cheaply, and it usually later descends into frustration or anxiety. Enduring happiness often comes after we have surmounted difficulty. That is, it does not usually have its roots in temporary pleasure. Pleasure often means doing what feels good right now; genuine happiness is based on doing what is morally proper. Nowadays, too many people go about trying to feel good rather than to do good.

As we have mentioned, we must become the change that we expect in others. In other words, all things change as we do. We should be asking ourselves constantly, "What do I need to change about myself to help others change?"

- We cannot be good leaders if we are not good followers.
- We cannot build teams unless we are ourselves strong team players.
- We cannot teach our kids self-discipline unless we are self-disciplined.
- We cannot enjoy a happy marriage if we are not good partners.
- We cannot have a strong network of friends unless we are good friends ourselves.
- We cannot develop a close community if we are not good neighbors.

A Chinese proverb tells us:

You tell me, I will forget. You show me, I will remember. You involve me, I'll understand.

A leader can tell people about character building, then help them take notice of others with good character. Most importantly, the leader can have good character, and always interact with integrity. Then he or she will be an excellent role model for others, and people will better understand what it really means to live with character.

Warren Bennis, the distinguished professor of business administration and founding Chairman of the Leadership Institute at the University of Southern California, explains how leadership is character, with which I fully agree. He writes:

I think leadership is character. Character is a word that comes from the Greek engraved. It's from the French inscribed. It isn't just a superficial style. It's got to do with who we are as human beings, and what shapes us. I also believe that character evolves as we grow and develop.

Bhishma's last instruction to Yudhisthira on managing the kingdom consists of his explanation that, ultimately, all things will be left behind. It is only *dharma* and our character that follow us out of this life. Ultimately, our real identity is based on our character.

CHARACTER IN COMMUNITY

Finally, as we look at character in an institutional or communal setting, we realize that an important part of acting with integrity is being trustworthy no matter what. One of the greatest blows to productivity and higher consciousness is people's lack of trust of one another, and especially of their leaders. When several people in an institution are prepared to take on the role of the trustworthy, a real sense of community can be formed. In creating such an empowering environment, each person commits to honesty.

Integrity engenders respect. There cannot be true love without respect in any case. We do not get along when we allow our own thoughts, feelings and desires to become more important than defending truth and our concern for others. If people are able to see truth constantly as a servant-leader does, they will learn to see things as they actually are. As long as we do not seek truth and do not strive to develop strong character, our vision will remain clouded.

Here is a wonderful quote that one of my colleagues, who has been managing an institution in Japan for over fifteen years, shared with me:

Coming together is the beginning, keeping together is progress, and working together is success.

Healthy coming together is staying together, and will only be successful if people attend to building strength of character, the father of all virtues.

The Power of Character, edited by Michael Josephson and Wes Hansen, emphasizes that real power is not knowledge but character. Here are eleven of their points:

1. The great philosopher Heraclitus said, "A man's character is his destiny."
2. Character is what a man chooses to do when the choice is not easy.
3. Just as the destiny of an individual is determined by personal character, the destiny of an organization is determined by the character of the leadership.
4. When leaders and individual employers have poor character, the organization will suffer.
5. It is character that determines how effectively we use our knowledge and skills.
6. It is character that determines how we respond to temptation.
7. It is character that determines how we proceed in success or failure.

8. It is not enough to even treat people well and use them well, but one must help people find meaning and fulfillment. This indicates a leader with good character.

9. Our leaders must learn to lead beyond walls and must also learn to become leaders in the community even to create community. It is not enough for a leader with excellent character to lead their own institution. But being loyal to their institution in its vision and progress they should be able to give healthy stimulation to the progress of the community or of the society in general, especially in the environments in which they are interacting.

10. Because of a lack of high character, we are now people who know the price of everything and the value of nothing.

11. Everything can be taken away from you, but only you can give away your integrity and good character. Integrity and good character are the window into the soul.

Also in *The Day America Told the Truth* by James Peterson and Peter Kim, there are some astounding facts that make us ask, "What has happened to integrity in America?" This book shows how character and integrity have been de-emphasized. Here are some of the statistics offered in the book [14] :

- 90% or nine out of ten Americans lie regularly. Moral fiber in the nation is seriously deteriorating.
- 86% of the people lie to their parents.

---
14   Peterson & Kim. *The Day America Told the Truth*, p. 48.

- 75% of the people lie to their friends.
- 73% of the people lie to their siblings.
- 69% of the people lie to their lovers.
- 61% of the people lie to their bosses.
- 59% of the people lie to their children.

Shakespeare counseled us more succinctly: "To thine own self be true." His point was quite profound, because when we are true to ourselves, it is easy to be true to others. We have low integrity because we are not first true to ourselves. This weakness extends itself into all our relationships and throughout our institutions.

GOALS AND A SENSE OF DUTY

Q: It seems that performing austerity without a fixed sense of duty is dangerous for leadership, because it could divert the mind and entice us to pursue a less spiritual goal. Without *varnasrama*, it is more difficult to fix the mind on duty. In many spiritual institutions we have tended to be "jacks of all trades" or to "do the needful," and to feel somewhat uncomfortable with the idea of specializing in one area of work. We tend to think it's less God conscious than being available to do whatever the Lord desires. Still, we're not always clear about what the Lord is asking of us beyond that vague idea of "surrender." Is it right in a spiritual movement to fix the mind on a particular duty? How does one stay fixed in that concept in a society that may not encourage it?

Also, would you consider the lack of having a fixed duty as contributing to a lack of personal and social integrity?

A: Austerity performed without a specific goal can sometimes not only create an unhealthy spiritual imbalance but can "harden" the heart. If one is not careful, austerity will not only bring power, but also the false ego that comes with awareness of one's power. This weakens the role of austerity in strengthening character.

People in general need balance, focus and even a project. If our intelligence, mind and senses are not engaged in healthy activity, they will naturally find themselves attracted to improper things. It is impossible to stop the process of thinking, feeling and willing, but we can work on making sure our thinking, feeling and willing are done with proper quality. The Vedic literature says, *param drstva nivartante*—give up a lower taste in favor of a higher one. That is, direct your consciousness in such a way that your energy is transformed from ignorance to understanding.

We find in management that people who have a part in bringing about a particular goal will then identify with that goal. When they identify with the goal, they will want to see success in attaining it. Therefore, it is important to bring people in on the pioneering level. The austerity associated with having to work for something from the ground up will help them remain committed as the project goes on. We must also understand that many crimes are committed by people with no skills, no employment, and, therefore, with low self-esteem. When people are engaged according to their propensities, we will find less crime in society. As people are engaged, encouraged, protected and cared for, they will also tend to value themselves more. This will also work to minimize crime, suicide and depression. Suicide is on the rise in almost every country in the world, and it has a lot to do with people feeling unprotected, uncared for, not valued and not properly engaged.

Regarding having a fixed duty, there is a special category known as "general assistant." This person may not have a specific duty but may oversee various things. Much of their work involves doing the needful.

However, people with this kind of service or work often find themselves frustrated, because they are not sure how to plan their lives or their work. They may overreact or underreact in crisis situations, since they are always so much at the mercy of what others do. Such persons are often unable to focus.

In a more structured organization, there is a healthy distribution of labor, so people know what is expected of them. There is no work that has not been assigned, and therefore no need of someone who must "do the needful." When people have a fixed duty, it makes it easier to hold them accountable for their work and, hopefully, to develop better character in the process.

DEVELOPING THE WORKFORCE

Q: Ideally, in spiritual institutions, all austerities should be aimed at satisfying God and attaining pure devotion. Often we draw a dichotomy between "pure devotion" attained through praying, meditating, chanting and hearing, etc. and the possibility of attaining it through our particular work. I think this is partly because we have understood that pure devotion is free of *upadhis*, or false designations. An *upadhi* is literally a shadow of ourselves, something we create that stands next to ourselves like a doll we then proceed to identify with. Calling ourselves leaders or followers, men or women, etc., is not working to free ourselves from *upadhis*.

So is there any point to austerity in terms of building our work ability? How do we perform our work as "leaders," if that is our service, or even as "citizens," without attachment? If we can remain detached from false identification, is it worth performing austerities that lead to something a little less than pure devotion—for example, a leader may perform some austerity (or pray) to attain strong personal integrity by which he will avoid becoming corrupt.

A: We, as material, metaphysical, emotional and ultimately spiritual beings, have personality. We should not try to abandon our identities or force others to abandon theirs. When people try to neglect each other's identities, relationships become artificial. There are those who deny people's identity by showing no respect for their gender, race, or ethnicity. Such persons may have good intentions, even acting out of what they feel is compassion, but they actually deny too much of a person's character. A servant-leader will study people's characters and propensities in order to best engage them in service. Compassion includes the ability to accept others' positions and situations without becoming distracted by them or impacting on them negatively.

When it comes to the workforce and trying to see everyone as the same, or when it comes to developing community, a servant-leader scrutinizes people's tendencies and tries to engage them accordingly in devotional service. To engage people in work for which they are not suited is low-class leadership. It will bring low-class reciprocation from the dependents.

Of course, when one is working for a higher spiritual goal, he simply wants to do whatever is necessary to accomplish the goal and does not worry so much about his own tendencies. This may even be true of those who are working for lesser goals but who identify strongly with the project. Such a person is prepared to do whatever the management requests of him.

While a worker may have this mentality, the management should maintain its interest in helping such persons become properly engaged. A servant-leader should look at such a worker to see his propensities, then find ways to increase his enthusiasm by fully engaging him in work that employs his talents and interests. In a time of crisis, when manpower is limited, a leader should make it clear that he is asking a worker to do something beyond his usual call of duty due to the extremity of the situation, but when things are back to normal, the worker too will return to his regular duties.

A leader who keeps a worker's talents and interests in mind when he assigns him tasks builds a relationship between them based on their individuality. Because of this relationship, a worker will not feel devalued if he is temporarily asked to work against his tendency during a crisis. When leaders continue to be task-oriented and place people in situations for which they are not equipped, they will continually find themselves experiencing one difficulty after another and will not be able to hold on to good people.

At the end of the day, a servant-leader who is specifically spiritually oriented will think how to offer everything to God. He will constantly seek to understand what is favorable for devotional service and raising consciousness. Srila Rupa Gosvami, a great spiritual scholar and practitioner of Vaisnava culture said: *nirbandha krsna sambandhe, yukta vaira yam ucyate*: "Those things that are favorable for devotional service should be constantly accepted and embraced. Those things that are unfavorable should be avoided."

As we maintain the mentality of a steward rather than a proprietor, and focus on our dependents' higher needs, we will learn more and more how to use everything in God's service. Thus, the leader and his dependents will attain a higher level of consciousness and purity.

LEADERS NEED GUIDES

Q: King Prithu received knowledge from his spiritual master, Sanat Kumara. This example of accepting a spiritual master is given as one of the requirements for becoming a proper leader. In today's society can someone become a qualified leader if they do not receive knowledge from bona fide scriptures and a bona fide spiritual master, master or coach?

A: Training is most important, but a lot of problems in organizations have to do with poor quality training. There are certain sensitive or technical jobs that can only be mastered through training passed down from accomplished workers. Similarly, there are certain things in the transcendental realm that can only be taught by those who have mastered them. In general, when it comes to higher spirituality, a candidate must prove his willingness to accept training in addition to being a recipient of blessings and grace.

In general, in any area of life, the quality of training normally determines the candidate's subsequent level of achievement and success. Look at the best musicians, artisans, sportsmen or the leaders in almost any field, and you will see that they were either trained directly by masters in their field or studied those masters closely and emulated their activities.

There are obviously exceptions to this rule. There are exceptions to every rule, and we can also point to a few examples of persons who mastered a particular skill without formal training. Often these exceptions are due to previous training, experience or maturation in the particular skill in a previous life. We have the example of child prodigies, where a young child sits down for the first time at a piano and plays beautiful concert music, or a person who has never had formal art training but who has incredible natural talent.

We see cases of successful leaders and managers who not only were not trained in the best schools but were not formally trained at all. In these cases, however, we see that such individuals have received inner guidance. As we study these individuals' activities, we will see that without knowing management theory, they employ cutting-edge technologies in their management style.

Those who wish to lead should always try not only to learn as much as they can from the highest sources accessible to them, but should make learning an ongoing commitment. Those who have already been trained in a skill but who do not continually sharpen their skills will become obsolete. Gradually, they will become a disturbance to others. A true servant-leader has a passion for learning. He also has a passion for teaching others, because he knows that by sharing his knowledge he will increase his own understanding. The sign of an empowered leader is that he will always have others training under him and other already trained leaders prepared at any time to take over various responsibilities. A leader who does not have a pool of leaders-in-training cannot really be considered a dynamic and powerful leader. A servant-leader is more eager to empower others than to control everything by his own power.

LEARN BY TEACHING

Training and teaching others is not only an essential part of divine monarchy and servant-leadership, but is essential to any healthy leadership. Recent investigations have shown that the best way to learn something is to teach it. In his book, *Teach What You Have Learned*, William Glassner presents these fascinating statistics:

- We learn 10% of what we read.
- We learn 20% of what we hear.
- We learn 30% of what we see.
- We learn 50% of what we see and hear.
- We learn 70% of what we discuss.
- We learn 80% of what we experience.
- We learn 90% of what we teach.

There should be a motto in all communities and institutions: "Teach what you have learned." Learn, read, research and hear the subject matter under study with the idea that you will have to teach it. Just imagine what happens in the mind when we study something we know we will have to explain to someone else.

In this age, our minds and intelligence are weak. Our memories are poor. We tend to quickly lose information we learned only moments earlier. In ancient times, hearing was one of the most important ways to learn. People's memories were sharp, especially people who practiced celibacy. Such students had tremendous mental and intellectual power. Even by hearing something only once, they would commit it to memory for life. There are still some spiritual groups who rely foremost on hearing as the best way to learn.

Although the ear is one of our more powerful senses, hearing no longer seems the most effective way to take in and retain information. Sight has at least equal weight. What we see tends to stay with us longer than what we hear. Repeating what we have seen and heard makes learning stick even better. Discussion involves the intellect; it makes us think about what we have read or heard. It gets us involved in the subject matter on a different level.

We can see how experiencing a given subject matter is most important—even more than teaching it—because while experiencing the knowledge, all five senses are involved, and therefore stronger impressions are left in the consciousness. This is why so much knowledge is now transmitted through seminars and workshops. Workshops generally give people a chance not only to discuss what they are learning but also to experience it in certain ways. This kind of learning stays with the participant longer.

An example of experience-based learning is role-playing. Role-playing gives a person a chance to assimilate various types of environments, along with various challenges, so that alternatives can be explored and responses made productive. Role-playing workshops give people a chance to develop insights from having verbal exchanges with others.

When we teach what we have learned, it also reveals to us how much we have actually understood of the subject matter. As we educate others on the material, it has an interesting way of impressing itself on our consciousness. Just as I am familiar with the points about which I am writing in this book. I have read about them and thought about them, but now that I have to write about them and share them with others, it helps me to think about them on a deeper level. From time-to-time when I hold workshops or seminars on this knowledge in different parts of the world, I feel myself gaining greater insight into what I am teaching.

It is most unfortunate that there are teachers who simply repeat the same lessons again and again without enthusiasm and without learning anything themselves. Not only does the student become bored, but the teacher does as well. The more the teacher is a servant-leader, the more he tries to both teach and learn at the same time, and thus serve both his own purposes and the purposes of those who have approached him for training.

Once again, this previous mentioned Chinese proverb is important: "You tell me, I will forget. You show me, I will remember. You involve me, I will understand."

As servant-leaders, we should provide the best training possible for those who wish to study under us; as students, we should find the best teachers under which to study if we wish to become experts in our field.

DEVELOPING GOOD GUIDES

Q: In the monarch systems of ancient India, the *brahmanas* used to control the royal powers and the royal powers (leaders) would reciprocate by giving protection to the citizens. Is a social system of ruling important to spiritual organizations? If so, what system would be most beneficial in an organization where the present day *brahmanas* may not be qualified to instruct the leader?

A: A good *ksatriya* (administrative leader), the divine monarch or servant-leader will always make provisions to support the training of *brahmanas*. Those persons most important to the running of good government are the *brahmanas*. *Brahmanas* are the wise advisors, the elders, those who transmit wisdom, the expert coaches, and those who best understand the people's needs. Without qualified *brahmana* advisors overseeing things (or those in some capacity as trustees, etc.), there will be no proper system of checks and balances. Leaders definitely have the tendency to go astray, and if there are no proper boundaries, then leaders will often abuse power or will lead from the back. They will become absorbed in power and will lose interest in the welfare of their citizens.

The *varnasrama-dharma* system of dividing society into specified groups is formed around the healthy distribution of services and labor based on encouraging people to work according to their propensities. In this way, people can render the highest service possible to their communities.

Sometimes we wonder which factor is most important in guaranteeing the success of a community or institution. All the factors are important. Now let us examine them. If those who are in the position of *brahmanas*—advisors, consultants, etc.—are not constantly available to offer guidance and supervision, if they are not constantly available to clarify universal principles and laws, then the administrators will not be able to maintain a principle-centered focus in their management. Over time, such administrators will begin to create policies based on self-interest rather than on the best interests of the institution or community.

In the case of Vena, he was an improper monarch, but he was invested with great power and influence. The *brahmanas* tactfully warned him to rectify his improper activities. The *brahmanas* and sages tried to find a way to encourage him to act according to higher principles. Vena blatantly refused their advice and stepped up his campaign to destroy religious principles. The *brahmanas* realized that their only reasonable course of action was to remove him. The *brahmanas* possess *brahma-tejyas*, the purification and strength of austerity and worship. Therefore, they had the power to remove Vena from his throne and to kill him with a *mantra*.

After removing him, however, they did not abandon their nonpartisan role as advisors and take over the throne. Rather, they remained onlookers and well-wishers of the kingdom. When rogues and thieves began to overrun the country, they could have again used their *brahma-tejyas* to control them, but they did not feel it was their duty. Dealing with the criminal elements in society is the duty of a ruler. For the people's protection against spiritual degradation, the *brahmanas* were prepared to remove an improper ruler. Otherwise, they did not see it as their duty to rule the kingdom.

Those who are going to oversee a community and offer it their good wishes as an advisor should be able to maintain a certain amount of equilibrium no matter what is happening. To do so usually requires that they do not become too hands-on. Rather, they should maintain their objectivity, and even more important, their sense of detachment.

THE FOUR SOCIAL CLASSES

As the *brahmana* advisor is important, so the *ksatriya* administrator is equally important. Without a strong servant-leader to actually execute the management work, society cannot function. The *brahmanas* and *ksatriyas* are interdependent. The *brahmanas* help protect the principles of the *ksatriyas*, and the *ksatriyas* protect the *brahmanas* by providing a society respectful of their wisdom and by offering them charity by which they can maintain themselves and their spiritual practices. Without the *ksatriyas'* protection, the *brahmana* class would die out.

The next social class is the *vaisya*, or mercantile and farming class. Without the *vaisyas*, the *brahmanas* could live with their ideas and the *ksatriyas* with their power, but neither class would have anything to eat. The mercantile class is responsible for food production and trade. Therefore, the *vaisyas* are important to the proper functioning of society. Without a strong *vaisya* class, the king would be unable to offer charity to the *brahmanas*, feed the poor, or, in Vedic culture, enact many of the prescribed religious ceremonies.

If the ceremonies were stopped, the *brahmanas* (whose duty it is to actually perform the ceremonies) would be unemployed, traditions would be lost, and the culture would gradually crumble. As the *brahmanas* struggled to maintain the traditions, they would become dependent on those who could support them—and be beggars rather than wise men—and thus lose their nonpartisan positions. Without the *vaisyas*, the monarch would have no one and nothing to tax, and his kingdom would starve or become overrun by others. It is the *vaisyas* who provide the raw materials for the two higher classes to live and prosper.

The last of the four social orders is the *sudras*, or laborer class. Often people misunderstand the *sudras'* role in society, and, of any class, this class has been the most subject to suffering under the modern-day caste systems of the world. In ancient culture, the *sudras* were considered the servant class in society, but were still accorded a respected and necessary place in the social organization. What we see in India today in the caste system is not the *varnasrama* system but a degradation of that system. This degradation has come about due to the teachings of unqualified *brahmanas*, who, in attempting to maintain their own social status, have created a false hierarchy based on birth rather than quality. This type of degradation has taken place throughout history, even within the spiritual orders. That is, the caretakers of the faith have become corrupted by monetary concerns and often by the *vaisya* class itself. Actually, one way to study the fall of any civilization is to examine the gradual deterioration of the *brahmana* class. When the *brahmanas* become corrupt, the rest of the society follows. The *brahmanas* are considered the head of the social body; where the head leads, the body follows.

When we study the setting in which the *Srimad-Bhagavatam* was spoken, we understand that King Pariksit was cursed by an unqualified and angry *brahmana*. While instituting proper servant-leadership, it is important that the *brahmanas* are properly trained. Unless the *brahmanas* are properly trained, the entire *varnasrama* system will become defunct. The leadership of *brahmanas* is extremely important to the proper running of a society. When *brahmanas* are unqualified, the other classes suffer, especially the *sudras*.

Sudras have simple natures and like to serve. A *sudra* is much happier being given guidelines on how to serve than having to decide on their own. Nowadays, under the deteriorated Indian caste system, people consider *sudras* untouchables.

It is beyond question today that to implement *varnasrama* without properly training the monarchs and the *brahmanas* would be a disaster. The monarch would become a tyrant and the *brahmanas* would use their positions to practically enslave the other classes. When the *brahmanas* become trained in selflessness, compassion and the performance of austerity and sacrifice, their wisdom remains intact and they are able to share it. Trained *brahmanas* will be a catalyst for the creation of powerful monarchs.

There should be more focus in organizations and communities on the power of training. Through ongoing training, better leaders will surface. This will produce the highest amount of synergy and symbiosis.

CAN MODERN LEADERS PROTECT THE CITIZENS?

Q: Giving the citizens protection was most important to King Prithu. He exemplified this by angrily chasing Mother Earth when she did not produce grains. In our world as we know it now, the needs of people are vastly different. How is it possible for a leader to protect all the needs of the people?

A: Protection is a must if people are to feel valued. If there is no protection, there will be no allegiance. Still, if a leader does not have a system to deal with lawbreakers, more and more people will begin to break the law. The servant-leader has the duty to make these systems clear so that people can be held accountable. If someone then chooses to break the law, he must be expediently and judiciously dealt with so that his bad example would not impact on others. The citizens must not be tempted by such unhealthy things.

When a mother cares for her young child, she maintains a constant vigilance over his environment. She watches for any dangers and immediately moves them away from her child, hopefully even before the child sees them. Children are notoriously curious, and are often attracted to things that could cause them harm. The mother must also look from the present into the future to see what her child will need and she must work to secure those needs. I previously mentioned that there is a difference between a servant-leader and a manager. A servant-leader is always interested in fulfilling needs rather than simply desires. This is one of the best forms of protection a servant-leader can give to others.

When those who choose to break the law are not punished or removed from society, the innocent workers are not protected. Not only does the law-breaker himself continue to pose a threat, but the innocent people are left confused because they do not know the actual standards of behavior expected of them. In this sense, people nowadays are less protected than people of the past. Few people know what standard they should follow in terms of morals and behavior. There are so many subcultures within society that normalize deviation. Some of them have become so developed that their deviations have become part of the mainstream. For example, pornography is one of the fastest growing industries in the USA, generating over $14 billion in revenue each year. At least fifty new pornographic websites are created every day. In the USA, gambling is now legal in most states, and it is estimated that 20 million Americans are pathological gamblers—that's twice the amount of ten years ago. Governments are filled now with bribery, and the black market is active. In some places, the black market activity is on par with regular commerce.

DEVELOPING GENUINE COMMUNITY

We must therefore remind ourselves about one of the principles of community: We should develop a genuine community rather than a pseudo community. In a genuine community, the individual gains more from his relationship with the community than he would be able to procure on his own. In a pseudo community, it is the opposite. If the community leadership does not offer protection from undesirable elements, people will not get more out of belonging to a community than they are putting in, and will thus not remain loyal. Most individuals who feel unprotected in their communities think they would be better off on their own.

Modern leadership needs a wake-up call in order to realize that leaders should be providing protection to their citizens or workers. Leaders should recognize that when people feel protected, they do not just give their hands, arms and legs to the tasks requested of them—they give their minds and hearts as well. Ultimately, they will help create a more dynamic and progressive organization.

Protection means not only understanding people's needs, but training people to fulfill their needs in a bona fide way. This is not a compromise. Protection needs to address the people's physical, psychological, emotional and spiritual concerns. If the leader is inconsistent or does not deal with the whole person, then the areas left unaddressed will remain vulnerable.

Sometimes spiritual leaders address only the people's spirituality and ignore their physical or emotional needs. They wonder why their constituents do not flourish in spiritual life. The great Vaisnava saint and scholar Bhaktivinoda Thakura explains in his *Caitanya-siksamrta* that there are four essential ingredients to a strong, viable community. If any of these things are not present, then the people will not be properly protected or cared for. They are:

1. The physical body must be cared for.
2. The mind must be sufficiently stimulated.
3. The cultivation of social interaction and well-being.
4. All of this must be done in connection with the study and maintenance of bona fide scriptures. The scriptures will provide guidance.

Bhaktivinoda Thakura also mentions that unless one is a *paramahamsa*, a completely pure and liberated being, these four areas are categorically necessary. Even modern-day leaders should be able to focus on these four essential qualities of a society.

LEADERS MUST SOMETIMES BECOME ANGRY

Q: King Prithu was a *ksatriya*, and also a devotee. Why, then, did he get angry and want to kill Mother Earth without first hearing from her about why she was withholding food grains?

A: Sometimes there is a misconception that spiritualists, divine monarchs or other types of servant-leaders do not become angry. This expectation is placed especially upon those who are spiritually endowed. But anger is sometimes a sign of love. A parent becomes angry at a child's behavior because they wish the best for that child. If the parent did not become disturbed when a child does something harmful to himself or others, it would be a sign that their affection was weak. Anger sometimes comes from concern.

Similarly, a servant-leader of any type cares about his followers. He has both faith in and affection for those under his care, and he wants to take care of their genuine needs. This is so much the case that he becomes disturbed when he sees someone doing something that degrades themselves or others. In such a situation, he may become angry. Here, King Prthu became angry out of affection for his citizens, who were starving.

We hear of the concept of hating the sin but loving the sinner. We must remind ourselves that God loves everyone, and that whatever love we feel is in service to God. There are those, however, who spend their lives trying to forget their identities as God's servants. A servant-leader sees such persons as possessing the highest potential, because he is aware of their constitutional nature as servants of God. But he also sees them as having gone astray. Therefore, he wants to bring out their natural, wonderful qualities. When something or someone interferes with that process, the servant-leader may become disturbed and do whatever is required to rectify the situation.

In the *Srimad-Bhagavatam* story about King Prithu, the king first questioned his citizens to see whether they were at fault for their own misfortune. When he realized that it was Mother Earth herself who was the culprit, he directed his anger toward her. This shows that the king felt responsible for all those under his jurisdiction, without insensitivity and without showing favoritism. It also shows that the divine monarch was quick to come to his citizens' aid when they needed him. Often we see that although the people are distressed, the government either does not come to their rescue or does not rescue them in a timely way. We often see leaders trying to avoid involvement in the distress of their subordinates. Instead, they try to maintain their good reputation and the assets they have accrued without having to deal with real problems. Understanding the problems of others takes work. It seems easier to offer patchwork solutions in order to keep the wheels of a community or organization turning, and to downplay or cover up the actual problems. Leadership in general is plagued with this kind of indifference. And to cover it up, leaders keep their activities confidential, only revealed to a precious few.

KEEPING TOO MANY SECRETS

A management style that must continually emphasize confidentiality is dangerous. One danger of too much confidentiality is that it minimizes accountability. It allows too many things to be hidden in closets and allows room for speculation. This attacks the culture of trust and love. Love is based on trust, and trust is based on open communication. When there is open communication, people can trust that the persons involved in management have the best interests of their subordinates in mind.

In the *Srimad-Bhagavatam* story about Krishna lifting Govardhana Hill, Krishna makes it clear to His father, King Nanda, that saintly persons do not employ confidentiality because they do not pursue relationships based on the duality of friends and enemies. Rather, saintly persons are everyone's well-wishers. Therefore, when such people need to rely on confidentiality, they do so with regret.

I do not want to negate the importance and need for privacy or intimacy. This form of confidentiality can be healthy. There are some things that are obviously meant for public consumption and other activities that offer more value to the community and to ourselves if they are done in privacy. Our focus here, however, is more on illegitimate secrecy—the conscious effort to hide or withhold pertinent information.

Gandhi considered confidentiality (secrecy) an agent of violence. He said it actually attacked peace, because there could be no peace without clarity and trust.

This is the information age, but even so, the world is full of attempts to block information from reaching the majority of people. Unfortunately, this causes antagonism, fear and doubt.

When a leader must base his management structure on secrecy, misinformation and half-truths, it can be dangerous.

Bhishmadeva mentions that there is a time for confidentiality. From that we can understand that there are times when secrecy should be maintained, especially if there is a lack of harmony in the environment. When threats and problems are intense, one may have to temporarily rely on secrecy to help reestablish order and justice, but secrecy should not be relied upon as a general practice in a mature, healthy society. In any case, managers should be open and honest if they wish to inspire an atmosphere of love and trust.

We should have high goals. To approach those goals, we should be careful not to embrace policies that detract from clarity, accountability and trust among members of the organization.

PRIDE & EGO

Q: King Prithu is an example of a powerful leader who was given all opulence, and yet he never became proud. Can modern-day leaders become prideless when endowed with opulence and numerous followers?

A: Pride and false ego are great enemies of those wishing to be leaders. My recent book, *The Beggar III: False Ego—The Greatest Enemy of the Spiritual Leader*, deals with this topic in detail. When a leader has followers and therefore receives praise, it is easy for him to become attached to the praise and to see himself as better than he actually is. There are many examples of leaders who were humble and dedicated during the early years of their administration, but as they became more successful, they lost their focus and became intoxicated by pride. Praise is like a drug. This is why the *Bhagavad-gita* states that we should be unaffected by both happiness and distress.

Perhaps that sounds strange. Perhaps it sounds as if a person who is unaffected by either happiness or distress is in denial. But a wise person is not affected by happiness or distress because when one is affected by happiness, he will work as long as there is praise and easy facility. As soon as these things are gone, he will lose his enthusiasm to work. When our actions are primarily stimulated by praise, we will not be steady when that stimulation is absent. Similarly, if a person is overly disturbed by difficulties, he will simply become depressed rather than learning from the challenges before him. He will also miss the opportunity to improve his service. Either extreme is detrimental for a servant-leader.

A servant-leader is always ready to serve. He will see all difficulties as an opportunity to grow and embrace a potential miracle. The more difficult the situation, the more eager the servant-leader is to see something wonderful develop from it. A servant-leader sees every new experience as a new opportunity to serve and glorify God. As far as receiving praise for achievements, the servant-leader knows that his success today can eventually become the source of his failure.

For many leaders of corporations and communities, their success is their greatest enemy. It is often true that the conditions that allowed them to become successful may not always prevail. It is typical that if we are successful by following a certain paradigm, we will attempt to be successful again according to the same paradigm. But times and circumstances change, and the same paradigm will not always work. Therefore, to rigidly follow the same course of action can cause one's downfall rather than his success, and if not an actual downfall, the rigid leader will be the cause of his institution's stagnation.

When leaders are proud, they will become overly affected by previous successes. When they have true humility, however, their thinking will be clearer and they will be able to more quickly respond to the opportunities actually arising. One affected by pride is more vulnerable than one who is humble. A proud person is vulnerable to the temptations of selfishness, intoxication, lust, envy and greed. When we study the lives of divine monarchs, it becomes apparent that even though they were invested with power and were extremely demanding when necessary, they were also capable of incredible humility—ready to receive feedback and eager to see how they could improve themselves in serving others.

This is another important area in healthy management: A servant-leader must be willing to receive feedback. He may even wish to establish a system by which that feedback is offered, so that he is guaranteed to hear it. If he actually wishes to serve his constituents, he must be constantly aware of their needs and experiences, and the best way to be aware of those things is to hear directly from them. In Bhishmadeva's teachings, he explains the need for sending envoys out into society to take note of what is actually going on. These envoys would then bring the information back to the king. Perhaps some would call these people spies, but their purpose was to gather information from the people, even without them knowing, and to bring that information back to the king for the citizens' own good. A divine monarch would accept this information gratefully, and then decide how he could implement policies that would better serve the people.

IMPLEMENTING VARNASRAMA-DHARMA

Q: Prithu's instructions to the citizens emphasized service to the Supreme Personality of Godhead and the proper execution of *varnasrama-dharma*. What role should spiritually aware people play in the introduction of this system to people in general?

A: The system of *varnasrama-dharma* is a Vedic system resting on the economic foundation of self-sufficient agrarian communities. The goal of the *varnasrama* system is to promote spiritual progress as the main function of human life. It is extremely important for us to try to reestablish such a system in the world. If we look at the statistics, we will see that cities are becoming more and more problematic, that the earth is becoming more and more polluted, that there is more crime, that there are many environmental disturbances (electromagnetic disturbances, the depletion of the ozone, etc.), that there is less space for both adults and children in the world, and that we depend on a false economic structure (falsity of the gold standard and an economy based on paper-pushing rather than actual trade goods).

It would definitely benefit people if they could take more control of their lives. When people live in agrarian communities supported by good leadership, they have the wonderful facility to grow their own food and to rely on more natural forms of energy. They are literally able to live a life of simple living and higher thinking.

Nowadays, people are engaged in complex living and low thinking. Therefore, violence is on the increase and people are moving further and further away from the natural environment. In an agrarian setting, we can learn to protect cows and other animals as part of our pursuit of peace and harmony. In such a situation, we would not feel the need to deny or conquer nature. People who must live in cities should, from time to time, visit rural areas and parks to rejuvenate their spirits.

My spiritual mentor used to say that cities are in the mode of passion and the country is in the mode of goodness. The cities automatically engender anxiety, frustration and gloom; rural areas make the mind peaceful and help us develop reverence toward nature and God. The country fosters friendly relationships between the various *varnas* and *ashramas*, because the people feel less passionate in the peaceful environment and more secure and supportive of one another. This encourages the leader, too, and enables him to carry out more of his prescribed duties. In an agrarian-based economy, the *vaisyas*, the farmers and merchants, would be taxed, and the monarch would protect them and their trade interests. Some of the taxes would be kept in a central fund for the benefit of the people. In that sense, the monarch functioned as a steward. Thus there would be a guaranteed arrangement to help people if there were an emergency. These emergency funds would be offered to people in times of need or as grants to help them develop themselves to better serve the community.

But without proper education and training of all the classes, the implementation of such a system would be devastating to society. It could easily be turned into fascism, racism, chauvinism or exploitation of one sort or another, especially by the monarch or the brahminical class. It is important that the members of the system be trained, and that is especially true of the *brahmanas* and the king, so that a wholesome society would thereby be created.

BEING RIGHT IN THE RIGHT WAY

Q: There is an incident described in the *Srimad-Bhagavatam* in which King Prithu performed an important ceremony. Although he was going about it in the proper way, he was convinced to stop his activities due to attacks perpetrated by Indra. Are there other reasons why a good leader would sometimes cease from performing a ceremony or a project that is otherwise beneficial?

A: This story reminds us that it is not just a matter of being right—we must try to be right at the right time, with the right knowledge and act in the right way. Of course, it is most unfortunate to be wrong. We can do the wrong thing at the wrong time or in the wrong way, or we can do the wrong thing in the right way, or we can do the right thing in the wrong way. What is most important is that we do not do the wrong thing in the wrong way, the wrong thing in the right way, or even the right thing in the wrong way, because when we do the right thing according to time and circumstance, the results are auspicious.

Knowing how to act properly according to time and circumstance is a science, and understanding this science distinguishes animated leadership from driven leadership. In animated leadership, we want to produce auspicious results all around. In driven leadership, we are only concerned with performing tasks. In business as well as in spirituality, we often want to focus only on the bottom line—representing our individual or institutional success. Or, perhaps we simply want to prove that we are right. This can be seen in preachers who want merely to defeat others (philosophically) in order to prove their own superiority. In the business world, someone might want to defeat the competition just for the sake of winning. In each of these cases, however, the vision is myopic and will not produce healthy, enduring, win/win situations. Synergy cannot be attained by minimizing others' significance. Synergy can only be attained when diversity is celebrated in a healthy way.

As the divine monarch has everyone's well-being in mind and is proactive, he always examines the consequences of his actions. This self-scrutiny will help him know how to do the right thing in the right way.

In the particular story of Prithu and Indra, Indra is definitely the offender. King Prithu was in the right. However, if he had continued to pursue his sacrifices, Indra's activities would have also escalated, Prithu would have been forced to retaliate, and the end result would not have been beneficial for society. Although Prithu was concerned about his ceremonies, he was more concerned about society. After weighing everything, he understood that he should give up his hope to complete the last sacrifice and leave Indra with his title of having completed the most sacrifices. Thus, King Prithu sacrificed his own desire for the welfare of all others.

Indra's pride and subsequent attempt to stop Prithu's sacrifice is an example of the cheating leader—particularly the cheating spiritualist—who will use devious means to fulfill his own desires even to the point of abusing a sacred culture. It is impossible for a leader to do the right thing in the right way if he is not selfless. If his false ego is too strong, he will be unable to respond effectively to produce auspicious results on all sides.

In addition to our false ego, or our identification with our material bodies, we have a divine ego, which is spiritual, loving, eternal, and full of knowledge. When our mind and senses are captured by the objects of their desire, so much of our divine identity becomes covered over and we become slaves to lust and greed. The false ego is primarily the active mind captured by lust, greed, envy and selfishness. It is hard to think and act on the needs and concerns of others when we are in the grips of such unsavory qualities.

A leader must also be careful to not present only rules or dogma, or even simply enforce laws. He must address the law's essence and be prepared to explain why he asks his constituents to do as he says.

Most importantly, the leader's own life must be his greatest message. The leader should show in his own life how he honors the law, but without fanaticism, and especially how he honors the spirit of the law, because he understands its essence.

BLIND FOLLOWING

There is a story from the Vedic tradition that reveals the danger of blind following and of not doing the right thing with knowledge, in the right way, at the right time. The story centers on a rather simple, poor man—a washerman, who had a donkey to help him carry heavy loads. A *dhobi*, as an Indian washerman is called, would pick up people's laundry, wash and dry it, and then return it to them. This man's donkey was dear to him, because it was such a help in his work.

One day, the donkey died. The man was so distraught that he decided to observe the same rites one would observe if a family member had died. According to the customs of his village, he shaved his head and spent some time in mourning. Then he went back to work.

This man happened to be the king's washerman, so when he approached the palace to collect the king's laundry, the king's priest turned to him and asked, "Why have you shaved your head?" With great emotion, the washerman said, "Didn't you hear? Sunanda-Gandharva died today." The name Sunanda-Gandharva is a glorious name and refers to one among the angelic class of beings. That someone would be given this name conveyed that he was of great nobility, if not divine.

The priest was embarrassed that he had to be told by a washerman that someone of apparently great status had died. He immediately went to the river, bathed and shaved his head to express his respect for the departed. When the king's minister saw both the priest and the washerman with shaved heads, he asked why they were mourning. The priest replied, "Didn't you know? It's such an important day today. Sunanda-Gandharva has died."

The minister was also embarrassed not to have heard, and he quickly went to the river, bathed and shaved his head out of respect. Being the king's minister, he thought, he should have been the first to know about such an illustrious person's death.

When the king saw the minister, his priest, and the washerman with their shaved heads, the king asked why they were mourning. The minister informed him that his great subject, Sunanda-Gandharva, had passed away. The king loved his subjects, even if he didn't know all of them by name, and so he too went to the river, bathed and shaved his head.

When the queen saw her husband and so many others with shaved heads, she too asked about the occasion. The king said, "My great subject, Sunanda-Gandharva, has passed away."

"Who is Sunanda-Gandharva?" the queen asked.

"Hmm," the king said, "I'll ask." He asked his minister to please tell him more about his great subject, Sunanda-Gandharva. The minister was delighted, as always, to render the king some service, but this time he asked the king to pardon him while he went out to gather more information. The minister went to the priest, but the priest didn't know anyone by the name Sunanda-Gandharva. The king's priest felt inadequate to present any details, so he suggested he ask the washerman, who was the original source of the information.

The priest eventually tracked down the washerman and conveyed the message: "The king wants to know everything about Sunanda-Gandharva. You must tell me everything you know."

As soon as the priest pronounced Sunanda-Gandharva's name, the washerman was overcome with emotion. He cried, "Life has not been the same since Sunanda-Gandharva left. We were so close. I thought of him at every moment. We wanted nothing more than to be together always. Sunanda-Gandharva was such a wonderful helper." By then, the priest was becoming impatient. "Please tell me clearly who is this Sunanda-Gandharva!" In an equally emotional voice, the washerman said, "Oh, Sunanda-Gandharva was my ass. He was a most wonderful donkey."

The priest was astounded. "You mean Sunanda-Gandharva was your ass? He was simply a donkey?" How could he go back to the king and tell him that he had shaved his head for a dead donkey?

Blind following. Do not be like a sheep. When one sheep jumps into a ditch, the whole flock will follow. If we do not have proper knowledge, we will tend to follow others blindly. If we do not communicate openly, or when we do things mechanically or ritualistically—and this happens especially when the leader himself does not have sufficient knowledge—we will together fall into crisis.

DEALING WITH DEVIANTS

> *"Lord Brahma continued: Stop the performance of these sacrifices, for they have induced Indra to introduce so many irreligious principles. You should know very well that even amongst the demigods there are many unwanted desires."*
>
> -*Srimad-Bhagavatam,* **4.19.35**

Q: How does this practically apply to us? If someone is disturbing a religious function, should he not be stopped? If nothing is done, it may appear to reinforce and support such behavior. In such a situation, how does a leader deduce what is the best course of action?

A: If someone is acting improperly, especially if their behavior disturbs true religious principles, then their behavior must be stopped or curtailed. If no action is taken, people will get the wrong message and may themselves engage in improper activities. In such cases, silence gives tacit approval. A leader must know what is right and what is wrong, and have the wisdom to judge what is right according to time and circumstance. If the leader is clear about the standard, others will be clear too, and everyone can move forward to embrace the higher standard.

Vedic teachings explain that an action performed in knowledge is always more powerful than an action performed without knowledge. For example, we can perform a ritual without knowledge, or we can perform it with an understanding of its underlying essence. Performing a ritual in ignorance still brings some effect, just as taking a medication without understanding its chemistry will still cure the patient; but performing a ritual with full consciousness allows one to participate fully in the cure.

There are always exceptions that one has to honor in administration and management, and leaders are sometimes forced to make decisions that would be otherwise unorthodox. In such circumstances, a leader should be able to explain to his constituents the mitigating factors that caused him to act in an otherwise unorthodox way. Even if the constituents do not actually agree with his decision, they will at least understand how he was thinking. A rule has its exceptions, but it is important that the ruler's instructions are honored and that the exceptions are understood.

Punishing a lawbreaker is not as valuable an example as is explaining the reasons for the punishment. Knowledge and understanding create a stronger deterrent than simply harsh action. It also helps the lawbreaker rectify himself, as he too comes to understand his mistake. A leader must be careful not to be too lenient in his instructions and discourses, because his subjects will not respect him and may even ignore him. It is also important that bad acts be examined, because without categorizing or evaluating them, no one will categorize or evaluate good acts either.

Therefore, a leader's duty is to reward the good and to quickly punish offenders according to the gravity of the crime.

The *Srimad-Bhagavatam* presents the example of King Pariksit. He was angry with Kali—the embodiment of our degraded age—and prepared to destroy him for the way he was treating the cow and the bull. He saw evil in his kingdom and he was prepared to do whatever was necessary to eradicate it. This was how he protected his citizens and stopped the spread of Kali's influence among the people in general.

Srimad-Bhagavatam, 5.13.14, offers basic concerns regarding *dharma*. Those actions that go against *dharma* are known as *adharma*. Forbidden actions are called *vidharma*. Forbidden actions obstruct us from following religious principles. No one should be obstructed from following their chosen religious system. (I refer to bona fide religious systems, and not those that contradict the universal principles of *dharma*.)

There are in fact religious principles that go against *dharma*, and that are temporary (i.e., not eternal) and relative. They are introduced by people of particular fellowships, usually with ulterior motives—whether racial, political, economic, or so on. Next there is *cala-dharma*, interpretations or speculations that miss the essence of true *dharma*. Another type of *adharma* is *upadharma*, new religions created by those who oppose Vedic principles out of pride. And there is the category of *abhasa*, a pretentious religious system manufactured by those who willfully neglect the prescribed duties of *varna* and *ashrama*.

It is the divine monarch's duty to both protect *dharma* and reinstate it when compromised. It is *dharma*—religion, integrity, right thinking, right action and excellent character—that will ultimately produce the highest good for the greatest number of people.

TRAINING PEOPLE TO RECOGNIZE GOOD LEADERSHIP

Srila Prabhupada's purport to *Srimad-Bhagavatam*, 4.16.4 states:

> *In the name of secular government, the king or governmental head remains neutral and allows people to engage in all sorts of irreligious activities. In such a state, people cannot be happy, despite all economic development. However in this age of Kali there are no pious kings. Instead, rogues and thieves are elected to head the government ... The*

> *rogues exact taxes from the citizens for their own sense enjoyment, and in the future the people will be so much harassed that according to Srimad-Bhagavatam they will flee from their homes and country and take shelter in the forest. However, in Kali-yuga, democratic government can be captured by God conscious people.*

Q: If people do not have the ability to recognize good leadership due to being so captured by the intricate web of illusion, how can the "democratic government" be "captured by God conscious people?"

A: Education is important. People need to experience a higher consciousness in order to work effectively in all areas of secular life and to help raise the consciousness of others. Without proper training, there will be no high achievers available to make significant differences in society. When there is a lack of good training, good role models and high achievers, people will simply follow fads and propaganda and will accept poor role models. People of higher consciousness are selfless and are willing to extend themselves to improve society. To achieve higher consciousness, we must first clear our own minds and hearts of unhealthy attachments and illusions, and then we must work on freeing the hearts and minds of others, bringing everyone through the window of clarity and truth.

One problem we encounter in today's society is that people are overly concerned about being "politically correct." They become bound by their need to be accepted by others, and so they become more concerned about other people's opinions and personalities than in developing their own. In this way, they become more concerned with that which works in the immediate moment as opposed to that which will endure.

All over the planet, citizens are rebelling due to heavy taxation and other types of policies imposed upon them by the government. They feel unprotected, their needs unfulfilled. In late March 2001, some of the citizens in Los Angeles protested due to an increase in electricity bills. Many third-world countries are filled with refugees due to civil and tribal wars and government repression. In some cases, innocent citizens are attacked by rebels or by the soldiers who are supposed to be defending the city against the rebels. The police often harass the citizens in such countries, and criminals are rampant during times of unrest. Even worse are the current terrorist threats and attacks. We can see how most difficulties in society are due to bad government and leadership. These leaders are stagnant, manipulative and exploitive, rather than divine and animated.

UNDERSTANDING POWER

Ultimately, when we discuss leadership, we are discussing power. To encourage good leadership, we should encourage good education and the development of strong character. Daniel Goldman, in his writings on group and individual self-deception, has provided us with several passages by prominent thinkers. What follows are a couple of examples:

> *It is a paradox of our time that those with power are too comfortable to notice the pain of those who suffer; and those who suffer have no power... To break out of this trap requires the courage to speak truth to power.*
> **—Elie Wiesel**

> *There are two kinds of corrupt members of an organization, those corrupted by power and those corrupted by weakness; i.e., persons who lack the ability to resist those corrupted by power. Neither of these are in touch with their consciences.*
> **—Eric Hoffer (social philosopher)**

Power often impacts people in devastating ways. At the same time, without power, our actions will simply be based on sentiment. Power means influence, resources, connections and insight. Without power, we will simply have ideas and goals but no means to achieve them. The ultimate measure of a leader is not how he acquires power but how he relinquishes it.

One of the ways leaders find to give power away productively is through coaching. Coaching is a method of shifting the culture of power over to others, unleashing the power within them.

There are many discussions of power—power to the people, absolute power, struggle for power, power politics, lust for power, abuse of power, balance of power, etc. Power is something that cannot be avoided. All interactions in this world involve the pursuit of a certain amount of power. In one sense, the whole history of this planet is based on people aligning themselves with different sources of power, both on an individual basis and a national basis. Living in a material body means lusting in different ways for power. I refer the reader back to my discussion on Bhishmadeva's instructions and his clear evaluation of the various types of power. They are also addressed as "power issues" in my book, *Spiritual Warrior III, Solace for the Heart in Difficult Times*.

Power employed with short-term focus is almost inevitably abusive and corrupted. Power should be defined as the opportunity to exercise responsibility. For some, power is a drug, a fascination. It is best to use power to develop trust among one's constituents. We currently have a power-driven culture rather than a responsibility-driven one. Abused power simply drives other people; power used to empower others creates a culture of responsibility. Wherever we see the word "power," we should be able to substitute the word "responsibility."

In *Leadership and the New Science*, Margaret J. Wheatley explains that everything is based on relationship. In the quantum world, it is not that only some things are based on relationship. All things are based on relationship. Life itself is simply the dynamic of various relationships. She explains that power in organizations is a capacity generated by relationship.

Martin Luther King, Jr. has made insightful statements addressing the human spirit and how to better develop a culture of genuine caring. He said:

> *What is needed is the realization that power without love is reckless and abusive, and that love without power is sentimental and anemic. Power at its best is love implementing the demands of justice. Justice at its best is power correcting everything that stands in the way of love.*

This is the real way to capture people's minds and to free them from unhealthy lifestyles and many illusions—by leaders using power to bring forth justice and to address and eradicate anything that interferes with the culture of love and trust.

GENUINE HUMILITY

Q: When King Prithu first appeared before the citizens, the sages glorified him, describing his wonderful qualities, but the great king did not accept their words, stating in *Bhagavatam*, 4.15.24-26:

> *How could an intelligent man competent enough to possess such exalted qualities allow his followers to praise him if he did not actually have them? Praising a man by saying that if he were educated he might have become a great scholar or great personality is nothing but a process of cheating. A foolish person who agrees to accept such praise does not know that such words simply insult him. As a person with a sense of honor*

and magnanimity does not like to hear about his abominable actions, a person who is very famous and powerful does not like to hear himself praised. My dear devotees, headed by the Suta, just now I am not very famous for my personal activities because I have not done anything praiseworthy you could glorify. Therefore how could I engage you in praising my activities exactly like children?

This shows King Prithu's humility, but it also raises a question about our everyday dealings. Often we praise each other or speak highly of each other in an exaggerated way. Most of the time it is not done with the intention to insult, but according to this verse it is an insult. Any comment on this?

A: Praise is not an insult. It is always important to reinforce the value of good leadership qualities. But it is equally important that Prithu did not take the praise seriously and that he was resistant to it. He set the example that leaders should accept praise, but they should always offer it back to the people and especially to God. They must be careful not to claim proprietorship even over praise directed at them. Rather, they have a duty to honor righteousness and to speak out against evil, sin and corruption.

A true leader will always feel grateful to his mentors and to God, and will not be afraid to give them credit. Such leaders do not want to receive credit for work they have not actually performed. Even when their performance is excellent, they tend toward humility, compassion and gratitude. Humility and compassion are the mothers of virtue. King Prthu was an emblem of such virtues.

EIGHT SINS OF LEADERSHIP

Gandhi spoke about seven sins that should be avoided.[15] This list should be important to servant-leaders as they organize and guide people.

Avoid the dangers of:

- wealth without work
- commerce without morality
- education without ethics
- science without humanity
- politics without principles
- pleasure without conscience
- worship without sacrifice

And I will add another:

- avoid religion without deep philosophy.

When there is wealth without work, it is easy to minimize the importance of commitment, responsibility and honest endeavor. When there is commerce without morality, the end will often be said to justify the means—rather than having a common standard for both means and end. Education without ethics will produce only sophisticated criminals, or students and academicians who know much but act poorly. Science without humanity allows some of the greatest minds

---

15   As quoted in *Leadership from the Inside Out*, pp. 87-93.

to concentrate without compunction on how to destroy the human race or any other species. Politics without principles will create leaders who will do anything to stay in power, regardless of its benefit for the citizens. Pleasure without conscience will allow one to pursue temporary sensual pleasure and miss the opportunity to seek more enduring happiness.

In addition to the aforementioned principles, I included the danger of religion without deep philosophy, because as my spiritual mentor once said, "Religion without philosophy is sentimentality, and philosophy without religion is dry, mental speculation." Religion and philosophy must go together if people are to understand the scientific aspects of spirituality. When people study science deeply, they will see its spiritual aspects; when people study spirituality deeply, they will see its scientific aspects.

ADDRESS THE HIGHEST NEEDS

Q: What if a leader is not actually committing sinful activities, but is not encouraging the highest from his dependents by his or her example nor by how he deals with those who are committing sinful activities? What is to be done?

A: A leader must uphold first-class standards to remind others of the highest goals. If such standards are not upheld, then he and others will fall prey to weakness. Given that human nature tends to be selfish and that people are often drawn into their own lower passions, if the leader does not stimulate his own and others' awareness of the higher self, he and his people will have a tendency to concentrate on the animal propensities of eating, mating, sleeping and defending—the work of base survival rather than self-actualization.

Abraham Maslow, in his discussion on the hierarchy of needs, explained that people have five basic needs.[16] The first is physiological. That is, food, air and water—all of which are necessary for survival of the body. Physiological needs are the first to be addressed. Once the physiological needs are satisfied or arranged for, people can progress to the second level of concern: the need for safety. Once people feel safe, they need to be affiliated with something. That is, they need to feel they belong to a group and receive support, affection, friendship and love. Once they have found their places in society, they can focus on developing self-esteem—self-respect, recognition and status.

Of course, after all these needs have been addressed he says then one can concentrate on self-actualization, which addresses our need to develop our human potential and to transcend the physical and mental limitations imposed upon us by our bodies. We can learn to connect more with the higher, spiritual self, ultimately realizing ourselves as essentially spiritual beings and developing our service relationship with God.

In the Vedic system, the quality of an individual or civilization is evaluated by which needs are being stressed in a list similar to Maslow's hierarchy of needs. In institutions, if the survival needs are not met, it will be difficult for the members to focus on higher concerns and the institution will not develop into something dynamic. If people are

---

16 Maslow, A. *Toward a Psychology of Being*, pp. 33-34.

not feeling safe, it will be hard to lead them toward self-actualization. This is similar to Bhaktivinoda Thakura's statements in the *Caitanya-siksamrta*, where he explains that without meeting an individual's more overt needs, topics of transcendence are irrelevant.

The Vedic system describes the hierarchy of needs as follows:

- *Anna-maya*: the organism is literally absorbed in the search for food and basic reproduction. Organisms functioning on the *anna-maya* stage barely distinguish themselves from others. Rather, they recognize only themselves and whether the "other" is edible or not.

- *Prana-maya*: the organism has moved beyond the consciousness of food vs. non-food, and can distinguish between itself and others, and its own species and others. At this stage, the need to defend (safety) becomes more prominent.

- *Jnana-maya*: the organism is developed enough that it begins to acquire knowledge and refine its thought processes, all of which take place beyond the actual physical need to survive.

- *Vijnana maya*: (also known as *ananda-maya*): the organism asks the questions, "Who am I? Why am I here?" and begins the philosophical search that will lead toward transcendence.

Many civilizations in the history of the world never evolved beyond *prana-maya*, which is also the level at which animals function. If we are honest, we will see that few contemporary corporations strive for much more, either. Much of the information available on management and corporate structure deals mainly with training people to pursue their most basic needs. Many management books make these problems sound like we are living on a battlefield when we address them. They speak about "tackling the problem," "capturing the market," "gaining full control," "never retreating," "eliminating the competition" and maintaining the combative mentality of "I win and you lose" rather than providing win-win solutions.

Other groups appear to have lost the ability to be proactive and cannot move beyond issues of safety. Some institutions do not cultivate trust in their members, and express fear at how managers and leaders use power. Their members fall into a survivalist mode in order to protect themselves from "the enemy." An empowered leader wants to encourage people to focus on self-actualization, and to do so, he addresses their physiological and security needs. He provides them with a model of good teamship, helps them feel a sense of affiliation with the institution, and provides them with validation to build their self-esteem. Naturally, people who feel validated want to develop their potential. From the platform of self-actualization, people can then move forward to *ananda-maya*.

Therefore, when a leader addresses lawbreakers or those absorbed only in the grossest levels of survival, he can connect with them at their level and try to raise them to higher consciousness by helping facilitate their needs. As a matter of fact, this is one of the main duties of a servant-leader; he must understand the actual needs of his people and how they perceive their own needs as well. Then he must help them constantly to move up the hierarchy and to develop themselves as fully as possible. When goals are not clear, people will speculate about what they should be doing and go off on tangents. A true leader brings out the best in people.

In that sense, we can say that every divine leader, or every powerful servant-leader, is spiritually oriented, because a true leader will want to bring his people to their highest level of development, which is inevitably spiritual. Real leadership is synonymous with arranging for spiritual growth. A servant-leader is always searching for truth. Truth has many levels, and if we pursue them, we will see that there are deeper and deeper understandings of the human condition. Ultimately, we will find that the deepest truth points us to our eternal relationship with the Supreme Lord.

FINDING TRUTH

The ancients present three interesting ways to evaluate the validity of something. They emphasize that when these three are in harmony, then we can trust the truth about which we are inquiring. These ways are known as *guru*, *sadhu*, and *sastra*. These days there is so much propaganda and relativism that it is hard to understand what is really the highest goal for each individual. Ultimately, *guru* (original spiritual guides) and *sadhu* (present saintly persons) will emphasize the importance of *sastra* (sacred texts). The sacred texts must be consulted for insights and even formulas about how we should live and what should be done in a variety of circumstances. Although we may consult these texts, it is important that we correlate our interpretation of them with the views of present-day scholars and adherents of the tradition that these texts represent. In our personal study and inquiry, we should examine the behavior and teachings of the founder of the particular system that we are following. We should consult a personal mentor and student of the texts, because he will know not only the texts but our own strengths and weaknesses and will thus be able to advise us how to best apply what we have understood.

For example, if we examine this point from the modern-day Christian perspective, the sacred texts would be the *Bible*, Jesus Christ would be the founder of the system, and the various Christian scholars and practitioners would be the *sadhus*. Christians should also have a pastor or priest with whom they can consult in the role of *guru*. If a Christian is trying to determine the best course of action, and his choice is not supported by *guru*, *sastra*, and *sadhu*, then he should reexamine what he has decided. He should not go only to the scripture for support, because it is easy to misinterpret the text, or to accept its instructions out of context. Scriptures tend to be deep, and we can often find many meanings within each passage. Sometimes those meanings even appear opposite from one another.

To clarify meaning in context, we must approach present-day saints. The role of saints is to protect the scripture and its tradition, to explain it in a present-day context, and to carry the eternal message forward. But we cannot approach only the saints, because it is possible for even a saintly person to become influenced by politics, commerce or sense desire, and to lose their spiritual integrity. So even when the saints agree with what we have found in scripture, we must still check both with the original founder of the system, and a current guide. For a current guide to actually fulfill the role of *guru*, he or she must be qualified by scriptural knowledge, spiritual mastery, and the ability and willingness to pass on what he or she has come to understand. For our part, we must be willing to be a determined student. It is a serious relationship in which teacher and student come to know one another for the purpose of moving forward on the spiritual path. If what we have found in scripture is supported by the saints but is not in line with what we know of the founder's actual teachings and life example, then we should not proceed with that action.

Very few modern institutions have authentic spiritual people at their helm. Neither do they have sacred texts to consult, or saints to emulate. Therefore, the emphasis in most institutions is on strategic planning and economic gain, and the deepest interests and needs of the members have been left far behind.

Actual spiritual principles are not only ancient but are universal laws integrally linked to the human condition.

In that sense, they are part of the human identity. We will also find, of course, that sacred texts, saintly persons and *gurus* are always linked to religious principles. If we see that something is in line with all three, we can usually trust that course of action.

Sometimes we see that a spiritual teacher recommends something different than the present-day saints, or different from the scriptural teachings, and when we look closer, we see that he is not actually in line with authentic spiritual principles. Great spiritual teachers come to fulfill scriptural dictates and shed more light on what previous teachers have taught. If we notice something unclear or even wrong in the theology taught by a particular teacher, we will usually find that the teaching does not actually line up with *sastra* and *sadhu*. We are not meant to follow spiritual principles blindly. If someone were to announce that he is a leader and therefore can throw out previous teachings and scriptures, we would feel the danger of his assertion. A person who does not want to submit to checks and balances is not a truthful leader, and this is not the mentality of an actual servant-leader.

Neither should we follow anyone who considers the tradition dead and the original bona fide founder an idealist. We do not need to re-create universal principles, or even spend much time interpreting what has been made clear through generations. The saintly persons should maintain the tradition, making any small adjustments that are necessary according to time and circumstance. They should never abolish tradition.

This point probably causes the most conflict between religions. If we do not understand the essence of all religious practice and the universal principles, we will honor only the externals of the tradition and mistake those externals for the tradition itself. Anyone who studies his own theology deeply will find that the universal principles can be shared with anyone else who is willing to study his theology deeply. To study theology deeply, however, we must honor *sastra*, *sadhu* and *guru*, so that all points are constantly validated against their own check and balance system.

If we honor the search for higher truth, this will provide a doorway by which we will find the common ground of universal principles. Only when we reach this common ground can we appreciate unity in diversity and free ourselves of sectarianism. Becoming free of sectarianism does not mean we have to abandon the details of our particular path. Rather, we should maintain our chastity and dedication to the path we have embarked upon.

Leaders who have found this common ground will not feel the need to force others into their way of thinking but will both be able to respect the truth in others' paths and will want to help them pursue their own bona fide theologies. In the ancient Vedic system, one of the divine monarch's most important duties was to ensure that everyone was following their bona fide religions honestly and with dedication.

This system of checks and balances can be examined in relation to any bona fide religious system. If we look at Islam, for example, we would see that if someone wanted to better understand a philosophical concept or conclusion, he would do this by reading scripture (the *Koran*, the *el Hadith*, and the *Muwatta*). He would also try to understand the teachings of recognized *mullahs* and *imams*. Then he would want to study the actions and dictates of the prophet Muhammad. If something is taught by the religious leaders but does not agree with scripture, then we can understand that such present-day teachers have gone astray. Similarly, if someone interprets the scripture in a way that does not agree with the understandings and realizations of present-day bona fide scholars or the teachings of Prophet Muhammad, then that understanding should not be embraced.

In every tradition, we should examine *sastra*, *sadhu* and *guru* to validate all our actions. When we are able to validate our actions, we are able to begin living for deeper truths.

FINDING KNOWLEDGE

Here is a list from such great Indian scholars as Jiva Gosvami and Madhvacarya about how such knowledge can be acquired. These are known as the ten *pramanas*, or proofs. The first seven are not really used by those who are interested in transcendental truths. Those interested in transcendental truth will particularly use the final three, and the last one is especially essential. I will give the Sanskrit terms followed by their English equivalents. Knowledge can be acquired through:

1. *arsa*: the statements of sages or demigods

2. *upamana*: comparison of one thing to another

3. *arathatti*: assumption
4. *abhada*: absence, or process of elimination
5. *sambhava*: inclusion
6. *aithya*: tradition
7. *cestha*: gesture or symbol; knowledge gained by someone making a *mudra* or sign
8. *pratyaksa*: direct perception
9. *anumana*: inference; to derive knowledge based on generalized experience
10. *sabda-brahma*: sound transmitted purely from divine authoritative sources

These are ten different types of ways mentioned in Vedic culture of gathering knowledge and truth. The divine monarch or servant-leader is primarily interested only in the last three. Most would have the greatest interest in the last process. Since the divine monarch's position was that of seeing from above and then passing on the information, and since the divine monarch is meant to be a representative of God on earth, a via medium between the material and spiritual realms, the divine monarch would avail himself of revealed knowledge. As his attention is focused in this way, it is quite natural for such a leader to keep his people similarly focused. Such a leader always maintains the highest goals at the forefront, while also tending the various needs of his citizens. Knowledge passed on in this way, through divine transmission, is transnational, transgenerational and, most importantly, transcendental.

AVOID OVERDEPENDENCE

Q: In *Srimad-Bhagavatam*, 4.17.10-11, the citizens petitioned King Prithu concerning scarcity, unemployment, etc. As it is the duty of the monarch to see that everyone is employed, how do citizens avoid an unhealthy over dependence on the king and his administration? And what about a leader who enjoys having others dependent upon him?

A: It is extremely important for a servant-leader to ensure that everyone is fully engaged and that the community is well-organized. He should not allow a few people to carry the burden of work; everyone should help. Neither is technology always an advantage, especially if it leaves many people unemployed. Of course, it can be argued that technology increases production, which in turn creates wealth. But this argument cannot be accepted in every case because too much is sacrificed. When machines replace people, people have no meaningful work upon which to build their sense of identity or even their loyalty to the community effort. The modern paradigm relied on by most managers does not concern itself with the self-esteem of its workers, and especially of those who are no longer workers because a machine has taken over their job. In the long run, people and communities will benefit by a minimally technological society.

SPIRITUALITY IN THE WORKPLACE

In our society we see more and more that people are fed up with pursuing careers. They want to pursue a mission. They want to use their creativity and their intuition to discover their true potential. Consequently, a servant-leader will arrange things in such a way that this becomes possible for their constituents. In order for these arrangements to be effective, however, the community has to be based on higher values. Obviously, exploitation cannot be the goal if the community is to become progressive. Rather, the servant-leader must help people feel a sense of ownership, an affiliation with the community and a sense of spirituality.

A Spiritual Audit of Corporate America, which is an amazing book written by Ian I. Mitroff and Elizabeth A. Denton, examines spiritual values in the workplace. It presents practical models for bringing people, body and soul, to work in a spiritual way—to imbue one's work-day with profound meaning. The spiritual technologies to which we are referring help in the workplace, such as accepting the fact that we are spiritual beings who are influenced by different kinds of *karma*, that the soul is eternal and is our essential self, that all bona fide religions are ultimately meant to bring us to associate with God, and that real spirituality helps us to recognize and honor other bona fide religious systems because there is one ultimate God who reciprocates according to our degree of surrender. The book provides hard scientific evidence how spirituality helps when maturely employed in the workplace, even though many managers feel that spirituality has nothing to do with work or politics. A servant-leader is not so deluded. He understands that spirituality is not only important, it is most important. It is through healthy spirituality that we see the real development of character and principle-centered leadership, and from this point, a more perfect community.

As most people in this country spend over half of their waking hours at work, we can see how important it is for them to be able to bring their entire selves into the workplace. This is especially true of their higher self. In this way they will not only be better people, but will offer more quality association and services in every area. To neglect or minimize spirituality is probably one of the worst things a manager can do to himself and others.

In using the word "spirituality," I am not referring to sectarian religious designations or particular dogmas. I am referring to universal principles, sacred knowledge, ancient wisdom, transcendental information and spiritual technology. Universal spirituality will have an empowering and harmonizing effect, whereas principles of sectarian religion will have the opposite effect, separating people who would otherwise be able to give so much more to their institutions and communities. Religion can often be dogmatic and easily corrupted with economic and political influence. But spirituality focuses on the essence. Spirituality will nourish the soul, going deep to the heart and therefore raising the consciousness. Religion tends to focus more on the external details, and thereby bypasses genuine unity, higher consciousness and self-realization.

CULTIVATING LOVE

The servant-leader's position is not to just keep people active or even happy with their jobs, but to literally get people to love the institution, the leaders and themselves. In my book, *Leadership for an Age of Higher Consciousness: Administration from a Metaphysical Perspective*, my first chapter emphasizes the power of love and how to engage its power and a "service perspective" as fuel for successful management. One of the main reasons I wrote this book was to address issues I had discussed with some of my diplomatic friends, heads of state and their associates. Since the book came out in 1996, over six of those people, all of whom were presidents of various third-world countries, have either lost their country's elections, been overthrown or been assassinated. Their failures have to do with points I addressed in the book and their inability to practice principle-centered leadership. In some of the international spiritual organizations of which I am a member, I have noticed that many leaders have retired due to frustration. Their frustration sometimes arose from their feelings of alienation in their post. They needed to learn how to love their dependents and to thus encourage their dependents to love them. They could have shown their dependents love by offering them work according to their propensities, providing more relevant spiritual guidance and protection and, most important of all, by the leader allowing his own life example to be his strongest message. One cannot genuinely lead with high character, confidence, compassion and courage without fully depending on and creating a culture of love and trust.

In the August 1999 edition of *Executive Excellence*, Chip Bell, a senior partner with Performance Research Associates in Dallas, wrote a superb article entitled, *"What's love got to do with it?"* Here are some of the highlights from his article [17]:

- A customer who likes you returns, but those who love you go out of their way to care for and defend you.
- A customer who loves you will insist that their friends patronize your business.
- A customer who loves you will not sue you.
- A customer who loves you will offer you candid feedback.
- A customer who loves you will be committed to paying their bills in a timely fashion.
- A love strategy means to treat every customer like a friend or neighbor, like the old attendants at the community store treated their customers.
- A customer who loves you will forgive you when you make a mistake.

A senior manager at the Marriott has this to say:

> *I want my customers to fall in love with our hotels. Thus, after he leaves, he will just be dreaming of returning.*

As mentioned above, when customers are in love with the services we offer and the way they are treated, and if they feel valued and refreshed, then they will love the institution,

---

[17] Bell, Chip. *What's Love Got to Do With it?* "Executive Excellence" ISSN: 8756-2308, 1999 Vol. 16, No.8, p.5.

community or business and its leadership. They will even be able to forgive the leader's mistakes more easily.

This is an area to which we would like to give more attention, because as we know, in all endeavors, even with the best of intentions, mistakes are still made. Our success or failure as leaders of institutions is often determined not so much by the mistakes themselves but by people's perception of the mistakes. Of course, for a leader, how he deals with adversity identifies his actual strengths and weaknesses, but people can push him to the limits if they are dissatisfied. If people feel the leader has their best interests in mind and has genuine affection for them, they are more willing to forgive. If they feel they have been lied to, manipulated or exploited, then often their attacks at a time of crisis will be vicious.

Jiva Gosvami, a great Vaisnava scholar, writes in his *Sri Tattva Sandarbha* about the four human frailties:

1. *Vihrama*: to be illusioned or deluded, an example is thinking the body to be the self or matter the essence of life.
2. *Pramada*: to be inattentive and, most importantly, to make mistakes.
3. *Vipralimba*: to cheat, lie, exploit, abuse, etc.
4. *Karanapataba*: to possess imperfect senses, which cause biased evaluations due to inaccurate or weak perceptions.

These four defects are present in every human being, and they cause us to make many kinds of mistakes. Therefore, it is said, "To err is human…"

But it is not necessary for humans to continually make the same mistakes. We are meant to learn from our mistakes and draw from our experiences. If we cultivate love and trust among ourselves, we will be able to forgive one another's necessary mistakes.

Just as people in the corporate world think that spirituality and the cultivating of love and trust is not really important when measured against the immediacy of maximizing profit and facing hostile competition, so there are those in spiritual leadership who see that in light of the tremendous work involved in transcending this world and approaching God, this level of culturing love and trust is extremely important. I have already explained some points mentioned in *A Spiritual Audit of Corporate America* and the benefits of spirituality in the workplace. Let's pause now and look at why the mode of goodness and the willingness to honor *dharma* is so necessary if we wish to embrace an eternal ideal. In the preface to *The Nectar of Instruction*, Srila Prabhupada writes:

> *In all spiritual affairs one must control one's mind and senses. If one cannot control his mind and senses, then one cannot make any advancement in spiritual life. Everyone within this material world is engrossed in the modes of passion and ignorance. One must be at the platform of goodness, sattva-guna, by following the instructions of*

> *Rupa Gosvami. Then everything concerning how to make further progress will be revealed.*

Here, the author explains that *dharma* has much to do with controlling the mind and senses. By such control, one can make ongoing spiritual advancement and overcome ignorance and passion. By such control, we will feel the benefits of the mode of goodness.

From goodness, healthy minds, bodies and emotions will develop, because goodness allows us to see with clearer eyes. From the platform of goodness, it is easier to understand what is to be done and what is not to be done.

THE MODE OF GOODNESS

I would like to introduce the thoughts of other Vaisnava scholars, since in this book I am trying to show the relevance of ancient thought in a modern context. In his commentary on the *Siksastakam* prayers, special prayers that summarize the essence of devotion, Bhaktivinoda Thakura writes:

> *One who chants inoffensively is overwhelmed with thoughts of others' well-being.*

By this he means that those who recite the Lord's holy names sincerely, avoiding offenses, will develop compassion toward others.

Srimad-Bhagavatam, 11.25.21 states:

> *Learned persons dedicated to Vedic culture are elevated by the mode of goodness to higher and higher positions. The mode*

> *of ignorance, on the other hand, forces one to fall headfirst into lower and lower births. And by the mode of passion one continues transmigrating through human bodies.*

This reference lets us know that the modes of ignorance and passion actually incarcerate us and cause chaos, deviation, disturbance and the loss of personal integrity. They force us to enter material bodies again and again, with no hope of liberation from the physical sphere. As we enter the mode of goodness however, we will be able to elevate ourselves to a higher position both in this life and after death.

In his purport to *Bhagavad-gita*, 14.10, Srila A.C. Bhaktivedanta Swami Prabhupada writes:

> *If one wants, he can develop by practice the mode of goodness and thus defeat the modes of ignorance and passion.*

Although there are three modes of material nature, if we are determined, we can be blessed by the mode of goodness. By transcending the mode of goodness, we become situated in the transcendental mode of goodness, which in Sanskrit is known as "the *vasudeva* state"—the state in which we can understand the science of God.

The mode of goodness is a launching pad to higher states of realization. Here the author states that if we are properly determined, we will be blessed by becoming steady in goodness. From there, we will develop naturally to pure goodness and be able to understand essential *dharma*.

The same author, in a discussion while on a walk in 1974 in Hawaii, said:

> *Without coming to the platform of sattva-guna, the mode of goodness, nobody can advance in spiritual life. This is a fact. Just like nobody can enter into the law college unless he is a graduate.*

This author's purport to *Antya-lila*, 1.92, of the *Caitanya-caritamrta*, states:

> *If in all of one's activities he strictly adheres to the mode of goodness he will certainly develop his dormant God consciousness and ultimately become a pure devotee.*

And, in a lecture given in Calcutta:

> *So we have to give up the association of rajo-guna and tamo-guna, passion and ignorance. Then there is question of progress. Otherwise there is simply bluff.*

MANIC LEADERS VS. SERVANT-LEADERS

Ultimately, we must abandon passion and ignorance, because they will degrade us, leaving us fixed in our own selfishness. Those who choose to remain in passion and ignorance cannot bluff about being absorbed in higher consciousness. If we want to learn eternal (*sanatana*) *dharma*, we must first practice regulation and cleanliness, humility and tolerance, and the other qualities of *dharma*. Before leaving his body, Bhishma made it clear to Yudhisthira that it is ultimately *dharma* that follows us, even after everything else has been given up or taken away. *Dharma* is the launching pad for transcendence.

There are those who are co-dependent and who take shelter of institutions or communities. They basically want to be taught everything and to have everything done for them. Such persons especially will be drawn to organizations with an autocratic structure.

Worse, there are those who will be drawn to leadership because they think they can become autocrats. Often, such people are manic and they like to feel in control. This is one of the dangers in modern leadership, and it drives people to take shelter in democracy. Manics will especially take advantage of having control over others to fulfill their baser desires. Instead of being servant-leaders, these people enjoy power. Manic leaders will be more interested in having followers than in empowering others. Ultimately, they will disempower the people with whom they come into contact.

Robert K. Greenleaf and others who teach servant-leadership constantly remind us that one of the servant-leader's greatest qualities is that, while being served, he becomes a better person. The more the manic person is served, the more of a tyrant he becomes. The servant-leader is accountable and tries to help others by honoring spirituality in the work place while keeping everyone engaged. He does not see the mode of goodness as a distraction but as important for creating an atmosphere of love and trust. Nor does he make people dependent in unhealthy ways, nor does he enjoy them as peons. He serves them faithfully, fully aware that his leadership position is his means to love them best.

LEADERS' PRIVATE & PUBLIC LIVES

Q: I was shocked by President Clinton's sex scandal, lying under oath and maintaining his position and popularity with the people. Also, there was the mayor of Washington, D.C., Marion Barry, who was caught smoking crack cocaine on video for the whole world to see. Nevertheless, the people of D.C. supported and reelected him rather than condemning his actions. In both examples, it seems that most people were not outraged by such actions but overlooked them and saw the leader as a victim. These degraded activities and lack of accountability are such accepted things that people are more apt to minimize the sin and focus only on the so-called good aspects of a person's character. This raises the issue of private vs. public life for leaders.

A: It has been said that the leaders make the people and the people make the leaders. After the people have been under weak leadership for some time, we see that their consciousness becomes more and more degraded, and this leads to the repetition of certain types of scenarios. Citizens who are not properly educated in higher principles will tend to choose or attract leaders who will support the lower standard. We see this in contemporary society. Leadership is gradually coming to mean management of people in order to make money. Such leadership lacks integrity.

Here are two cases in point: the former mayor, Marion Barry, and the former U.S. president, Bill Clinton. Neither of these leaders were servant-leaders, although they were good managers and were able to provide for their constituents' physical needs. This is all the people really asked of them. These needs are what people consider their personal rights. These leaders also felt that they had a right to a private life that should not be closely examined nor considered a disqualification of their ability to perform their public duty. In many ways, a leader's private life is even more important than his public life. A leader's public life is often more of a performance. It is the private life that gives us a greater indication of his consciousness.

A leader's actual consciousness will dictate how he forms policies. Mahatma Gandhi emphasized that leaders must have a uniform standard of conduct. One cannot act improperly in their private life and consider it all right because one is a good manager. If one is improper in one area of life, that activity will certainly cloud other areas of life. This is why I am emphasizing the importance of character development.

The *Vedas* mention *acaryavan puruso veda*: one who knows the *acarya* and the *Vedas* knows what is what. And inasmuch as the real *acarya* (leader) is living the truth, he becomes a role model for other truth-seekers. The *Vedas* also mention *acara* and *pracara*, that the actions and speech of true servant-leaders are similar. That is, he or she does not act one way while saying something else. They are not hypocritical.

Since people themselves have such little integrity or wholeness, their lives are fragmented into political lives, cultural lives, institutional or business lives, social lives and religious lives. By the end of the day, they are often confused about their actual identity. They have different standards of conduct in all their different roles. It is no wonder that so many people today are having mental breakdowns.

There are three areas to which leaders often fall prey: illicit sex, intoxication and a lack of financial accountability. In the case of Marion Barry, he did wonderful things for his constituents, but he was ruined by his use of illicit drugs and his support of the drug industry. Considering that drug abuse is one of the worst problems facing the youth in this country, it is a betrayal of trust to have a mayor of a major city involved in the same activity.

In the case of President Clinton, he also betrayed the nation's trust. In a sense, he indulged in incest. That is, he was a caretaker or father to his people, and the girl involved was young enough to be his daughter. If he had been a normal parent or even an average leader of almost any organization in the world, there would be no way for him to maintain his position.

One of my students, who was highly placed in the U.S. Marines, told me that if she or any of her junior staff members or officers did something even half as serious as what President Clinton did, she would have lost her job in the military. Here, President Clinton, her commander-in-chief, could have an adulterous affair, remain in office and continue to be supported by the American people. She saw this as a contradiction to the meaning of true leadership.

It has since been shown that his improper actions have led others to engage in similar activities. His example of indulging in immediate sense enjoyment rather than considering the example he would set for others is just the type of mentality that is creating counterfeit leaders all over the world and degrading civilization.

We need to sound a wake-up call in order to tell people that it is the time for real, animated leadership rather than driven leadership. We need leaders who are prepared to lead from the inside out.

Aside from the bad image Clinton's actions gave our country, the taxpayers spent an enormous amount—over forty million dollars—on the investigation. Clinton spent ten million on his defense. Fifty million dollars was spent on a case that directly showed a lack of integrity in the leadership. Just imagine what a good leader could have done with fifty million dollars to help education, social welfare and other such projects.

Aside from the money, consider how Clinton lied to over one billion people. Many feel that he did not even regret his actions but only regretted misleading them. Most managers would have lost their jobs for having sex with an aide young enough to be his daughter, but many people in the U.S. and the White House did not see it as a very serious crime.

However, many people felt betrayed to see someone in a position of leadership abuse his power and then deny it. Adultery is itself a lie, an act of betrayal, so for those who think an adulterer can call a press conference to enlighten others about the truth are facing a contradiction.

If we examine the history of the U.S. presidency, we will see that acts of promiscuity are common. Warren G. Harding had sex in a White House closet with a woman thirty years younger than himself. President John F. Kennedy also had sex in the closet, explaining to the woman that Harding had done this previously. Others have had sex in the White House swimming pool, and history has revealed that there have been many illicit relationships carried out in the building established to represent the American people. This is an example of how one leader created a model that another leader followed.

President Johnson climbed in bed with an aide while his wife slept in the next room. Franklin Roosevelt had affairs with his wife's secretary. President Grover Cleveland was frequently attacked by Republicans for his adulterous activities and his producing an illegitimate child. These immoral activities in high places by leaders who are supposed to be stewards who protect the citizens happen in every aspect of leadership. The worst examples, of course, occur in cases where the leader is a religious leader—priests, nuns, *imams* or *gurus*. Even some of the popes have engaged in illicit activities, despite their lifetime vows of celibacy.

Much of this infidelity has to do with lust taking precedence over love. In our society, people are confused about what love is. Since people view love in terms of their sense gratification, the idea of love easily degrades into lust.

This is one of the reasons why incest is also on the rise. People are being programmed to think through their genitals. We are constantly bombarded by the media and advertisers, especially in the Western countries, with sexually stimulating material. My book, *Spiritual Warrior II: Transforming Lust into Love*, discusses this topic in detail. I recommend that readers look at the first chapter, "Sex and the Leadership Crisis," to learn more about this topic.

DANGERS OF BLIND ENJOYMENT

People nowadays are trying to experience personal enjoyment at any cost. The following story emphasizes the danger of trying to have one's senses endlessly stimulated.

A man who was walking in the forest saw a tiger. The tiger began to chase him. As he was running, he saw a well covered by grass. He saw two branches growing out from the walls of the well. Holding onto them, he lowered himself into the well to save himself from the tiger.

However, the tiger saw him enter the well. It stopped at the edge and leaned over. The man looked down to see if he could change his position in the well and noticed two cobras, their hoods extended, at the bottom of the well. His legs were dangling over the serpents.

Then two rats came, one black and one white, and began nibbling at the branches he was holding. The rats signify night and day, the tiger death, and the serpents, life's difficulties.

What a precarious situation this man is in! There are dangers above and dangers below. Above him on a tree, he saw a beehive, dripping with honey. As he looked up, he realized that the honey was dripping in such a way that if he stuck out his tongue, he could just catch a few drops. The man became preoccupied by trying to catch the honey on his tongue. Every now and then he would manage to catch a drop. He began to enjoy the honey's sweet taste and he soon forgot the dangers he faced.

The temporary pleasures that people experience amid unlimited dangers normally preoccupy them. This is called denial of reality.

OUR HIGHER PURPOSE

Life has a higher purpose, but few people know what it is or even that it exists. Most are only concerned with improving the *anna-maya* and *prana-maya* concerns of eating, sleeping, mating and defending. Or they become stuck at the earlier stages of maturation that both Maslow and the Vedic system present. That is, they expend all their energy on fulfilling physiological needs and the need for affiliation without ever understanding anything more.

However, while expending so much energy, old age creeps up and death soon follows. Whatever one worked so hard to acquire in the material realm is then lost. All that is left, all that is carried away from this body with the individual soul, are the values he imbibed and the composite of the deeds he performed. If one spent his life only trying to satisfy the physical body, he has certainly cheated himself and those around him while never actually experiencing human life.

Real living means connecting with our real identity, the higher identity in its connection with God. From this point, we can experience real love. However, we cannot experience such a high level of love if we are too interested in materialism and the externals of physical life. When we remain on the platform of physical survival, our minds and hearts are fragmented by unlimited desires. We will not be capable of feeling the depths of love. Love is based on wholeness, selflessness and the ability to share our essence in very genuine ways.

As long as we continue to pursue physical and mental pleasure at any cost, we will continue to literally enjoy ourselves to death. Now we see that people are trying to entertain themselves in unhealthy ways and that they are speeding up the process of their lives and dying younger. Studies show that more people are dying from self-imposed illness—illness imposed by unhealthy lifestyles—than from any other diseases. More people are dying from illnesses related to stress, lack of exercise, depression, smoking, drinking, drugs, illicit and unhealthy mixtures of pharmaceutical drugs and diseases caused by sexual promiscuity than ever before. But what can be done when unprincipled leadership sets an example that encourages others to aim for nothing higher?

MATERIALISTIC GURUS

Among the leaders are those thinkers—scientists and philosophers—who, while making some beneficial contributions to society, have somewhat hurt human development by focusing on gross materialism and denying the existence of God. These teachings allow people to be more aggressive and less accountable for their moral decisions. It has focused the meaning of human life on the individual's self-centered pleasure rather than on social benefit or transcendental life. I call these people "materialistic *gurus*."

One such person is Francis Bacon. He played a significant role in separating man from nature, encouraging humankind to exploit nature as he placed more emphasis on science and technology than on God as the creator. Adam Smith is another such person, who made an interesting contribution by focusing on human greed and selfishness, stressing how these qualities are the basis of any strong economy. He suggested that encouraging people to increase their greed and selfishness would actually strengthen the market.

Another "materialistic *guru*" is Charles Darwin, who gave the world his theory of survival of the fittest. In many ways, he reduced the meaning of human life to biology and allowed us, for the first time, to understand that we were simply sophisticated animals fighting for territory like any other animals. Then we have Karl Marx, who presented a philosophy of dialectical materialism, foreseeing the downfall of capitalism and presenting the model of a classless society, but one in which God had no place.

Then we have Sigmund Freud, who contributed significantly to our understanding of human psychology, but who had no basic interest in God. At last, I would like to mention Machiavelli, who was most gross in his theory about how we should view selfishness as good. He also presented the message of shrewdness, which focused on using people for one's own pleasure.

Do we realize how these people's teachings have been spread around the globe? Millions of people have been influenced directly or indirectly by their philosophies. It is rare to find leaders who can see and practice the higher meaning of human life.

The propagation of these teachings helps us to understand that the leader makes the age far more than the age makes the leader. In other words, the quality of leadership is responsible for determining the collective consciousness of the citizens.

A CIVILIZATION IN DECLINE

J. Bradley Keena gives ten points that indicate the demise of a culture or civilization.[18] I would like to end by looking closely at these ten points, because we are seeing signs indicating the demise of our own culture.

---

18   Keena, J. Bradley, *Ten Signs of a Culture's End*

1. A Society Which no Longer Worships or Acknowledges God: As we see in all areas of life including strong positions of atheism and materialism.

2. Decline of the Family: Divorce is at an all-time high, no-fault divorce laws are being enacted everywhere, mothers working and fathers not at home.

3. Low View of Life: Abortion as a right, partial-birth abortions, assisted suicide, euthanasia and genetic engineering.

4. Prevalence of Base and Immoral Entertainment: Like Rome with its gladiators, TV and cinema treat perversion as normal.

5. Increase of Violent Crime Among Young People: Gangs, violent sports (i.e., one newspaper article called the fighting that goes on during soccer matches "warlike"), and cities are becoming like battle zones. The hospital emergency rooms are overrun with trauma cases daily.

6. Declining Middle Class: Middle class is becoming more defined as the working poor.

7. Insolvent Governments: Cannot manage a balanced budget.

8. A Government that Lives off of a Society's Moral Decay: Agencies that foster society's decline; that is, lottery, beauty pageants, and some might even question the FBI and CIA. Perhaps those agencies are headed for this category.

9. The Ruling Class Loses It's Will: Such as those who we just discussed. Previous presidents and others who say one thing and act differently, and who lack fidelity, morality, proper ethics, and who assault the minds of pious people.

10. Failure of People to See What Is Happening, even though it is obvious: Even though all the other nine categories are present in society, the majority of people cannot understand the implications or the dangers. The danger looms from above and below, but the people are lost in trying to catch a few drops of honey.

Keena observes that these ten categories are becoming so clear that our culture is in a serious state of deterioration. Therefore, we ask you, our readers, to look closer, to look for animated servant-leaders who have the passion to help others; leaders who are deep lovers, who know how to use money and power to empower others, who help people feel happy and secure, and who create lasting value. Servant-leaders are philosophical because they are always seeking truth. They lead from the inside out; with the clarity that character is power. They are principle-centered, because they rely on universal principles and laws rather than relativisms. They are powerful visionaries because they are concerned with a culture of excellence that continues to provide for those they love. They keep people engaged according to their propensities, realizing that this is the best way to honor their existence. They are expert at delegation and empowerment because they see themselves as stewards rather than autocrats. Most important, their life is a message to others, and they leave a culture of enduring excellence behind them. To properly honor such leaders, we must understand the importance of all of these qualities.

CONCLUSIONS

In order to have better organizations, communities or institutions, we must not only look for, but demand, higher performance from our leaders. The best way to do this is for people to work on their own character. As they develop, they will naturally both demand and engender caretakers of a higher caliber.

How can people work on their own character in a society filled with unhealthy materialism and so many other problems? They themselves must lead from the inside out.

As we look at management systems, we want to become leaders who are wise and able to make decisions. We want to build teams, define cooperative roles, achieve as much as we can, and set high goals. We especially want to be concerned with the whole person by connecting with timeless principles that direct us more and more to the interior.

For example, we have the science of astronomy, but the interior focus is astrology. We have mathematics, but the interior focus is numerology. We have physics, but the interior focus is metaphysics. We have chemistry, but the interior focus is alchemy. We have allopathic medicine, but the interior focus is naturopathy. We have psychology, but the interior focus is parapsychology. We have religion, but the interior focus is spirituality.

We conclude, after looking at the teachings of Bhishmadeva and King Prithu, that the ancient wisdom is still valid, and that sacred rule can help bring humankind back on track toward self-realization and proper social interdependence.

It will be difficult to reverse current social trends, but each person is important and can make a difference. Effort is important, as is grace. We should always work as if our success depends upon our own work, while we know that our success is actually dependent on God's grace. We should not be among those who wait for God to solve all our problems. God is waiting for us, and He has no favorites. He is an equal-opportunity employer.

Each individual should do his or her best because each individual is a leader. Everything we do affects our children and, in that sense, we are stewards of their future. The choices we make now will determine what choices those who come after us will have available to them. Will we offer them an inheritance based on a lifestyle that is causing our society's demise? Or will we turn things around? The decision is up to each of us. It is wonderful that we can be helped by the excellent teachings of Bhishmadeva, which are some of the

CONCLUSIONS

earliest teachings on leadership on earth. It is also wonderful that we can be inspired by the divine rule of a king like Prithu. He was truly a rare leader who had no desire other than to lead his citizens toward their ultimate good.

We end with the words of Gandhi:

> *We must become the change that we expect to see in the world.*

This is the secret for leadership in an age of higher consciousness.

EPILOGUE

BY PROFESSOR MICHAEL WHITTY

We are in a titanic battle between love and fear. Too much fear and not enough love. Finally, principles of love are being seriously presented as models for the just and good organization that we all seek to serve as part of our life legacy. This book is part of our organizational journey to the possible human—A book by a servant-leader discussing our role in becoming visionary leaders for the possible future.

The world faces the ongoing challenge of raising consciousness, developing skills and taking action. *Leadership for an Age of Higher Consciousness II* continues to not only provide deeply spiritual insights on empowerment and virtuous management but it allows an honest, open dialogue between religion, consciousness and the world of mundane administration. All this is badly needed in an age of stress, confusion and desperation.

The writings of His Holiness B.T. Swami seek to liberate the corporate soul and build visionary organizations based on visionary leaders. *Leadership for an Age of Higher Consciousness* is a bold, practical blueprint for moving business to the next evolutionary level. This book provides a paradigm-shifting look at how leaders can harness the creative potential of people and organizations. The author concisely develops and explains Vedic scripture as timeless wisdom for modern life.

Since corporations rule the world and the power elites are much like the kings of the ancient past, the timeless wisdom of Eastern (and Western) philosophy is once again very relevant to the character and policy orientation of leadership. The world needs philosophy to provide balance—otherwise we will see money and power continue to overshadow the common good. B.T. Swami provides a modern vision for leadership based on a philosophy of love and human unity. This book signals the road less traveled by a cynical and selfish world. But the creed of greed has outlived its usefulness to the planet. Now visionary leaders must offer a new paradigm for life, work and human destiny. There is a new stirring of soul in the workplace. This book is a leading part of the future trend toward servant-leadership and higher consciousness.

B.T. Swami is a truly unique spiritual scholar. He has integrated the wisdom of ancient Vedic teachings on leadership with the theories of modern management and leadership.

This is one of the very few successful attempts to reach the contemporary reader with a practical psychology for leaders in a spiritual context. This book is a bridge between inner life and outer work. You have found a rare book!

Yes, this book is well suited for spiritual seekers looking for hope in a complex, modern organizational world. The significant body of spiritual-minded scholars of organizational theory and transformation will discover valuable insights into Vedic scripture. Hopefully, this cross-fertilization of East and West will lead to more integral studies of religion and organizational theory. There is a growing trend toward servant-leadership and a spiritual future for work—a new spiritual meaning for work itself.

Professor Michael Whitty
College of Business, University of Detroit Mercy
Co-editor, Work and Spirit: A Reader of New Spiritual Paradigms for Organization

GLOSSARY

Acarya: A spiritual master who teaches by his own example, and who sets the proper religious example for all human beings.

Anga Maharaja: The father of King Vena.

Arjuna: The third son of Pandu and intimate friend of Lord Krishna. After Pandu was cursed by a sage, Kunti used a special *mantra* to beget children and called for the demigod Indra. By the union of Indra and Kunti, Arjuna was born. In his previous life he was Nara, the eternal associate of Lord Narayana. Krishna became his chariot driver and spoke the *Bhagavad-gita* to him on the Battlefield of Kuruksetra.

Bhagavad-gita: A seven hundred verse record of a conversation between Lord Krishna and His disciple, Arjuna, from the *Bhisma Parva* of the *Mahabharata* of Vedavyasa. The conversation took place between two armies minutes before the start of an immense fratricidal battle. Krishna teaches the science of the Absolute Truth and the importance of devotional service to the despondent Arjuna, and it contains the essence of all Vedic wisdom.

Bhaktivinoda Thakura: (1838-1915) The great-grandfather of the present-day Gaudiya Math movement, the father of Srila Bhaktisiddhanta Sarasvati, and the grand-spiritual master of His Divine Grace A.C. Bhaktivedanta Swami Prabhupada. Srila Bhaktivinoda Thakura was a responsible magistrate, temple officer and a householder, yet his service to the cause of expanding the mission of Lord Caitanya Mahaprabhu is unique. He has written many books on the philosophy of Lord Caitanya Mahaprabhu.

Bharata: Half-brother of Lord Rama, he ruled Ayodhya when Lord Rama was in exile.

Bharata Maharaja: An ancient king of India and a great devotee of the Lord from whom the Pandavas descend. The son of King Dusyanta who renounced his kingdom and family at an early age.

Bhishmadeva: The grandfather of the Pandavas, and the most powerful and venerable warrior on the Battlefield of Kuruksetra. The noble general respected as the "grandfather" of the Kuru dynasty. He is recognized as one of the twelve *mahajanas*: authorities on devotional service to the Lord. He was given a boon to leave his body any time he pleased, consequently he decided to leave while laying on a bed of arrows in full view of Lord Sri Krishna.

Brihaspati: The spiritual master of King Indra and chief priest for the demigods.

Caitanya Mahaprabhu: (1486-1534) Lord Krishna in the aspect of His own devotee. He appeared in Navadvipa, West Bengal, and inaugurated the congregational chanting of the holy names of the Lord to teach pure love of God by means of *sankirtana*. Lord Caitanya is understood by Gaudiya Vaisnavas to be Lord Krishna Himself.

Chanakya Pandita: The *brahmana* advisor to King Candragupta, who was responsible for checking Alexander the Great's invasion of India. He is a famous author of books containing aphorisms on politics and morality.

Dharma: Religious principles; one's natural occupation or duty. The capacity to render service, which is the essential quality of a living being. The occupational eternal duty of the living entity, regarded as inseparable from the soul himself (*sanatana-dharma*).

Dhobi: A man who washes clothes.

Dhruva Maharaja: A great devotee who at the age of five performed severe austerities and realized the Supreme Personality of Godhead. He received an entire planet, the Pole Star.

Duryodhana: The firstborn and chief of the evil-minded one hundred sons of Dhritarastra, and chief rival of the Pandavas. He was a wicked *asura* (ungodly person) by birth. He became envious of the Pandavas and tried in many ways to kill them. It was for the sake of establishing Duryodhana as king of the world that the Kurus fought the Battle of Kuruksetra. He was killed by Bhima, who broke Duryodhana's thighs on the last day of the battle of Kuruksetra.

Govardhana: A large hill dear to Lord Krishna and His devotees. Krishna held it up for seven days to protect His devotees in Vrindavana from a devastating storm sent by the demigod Indra.

Gunas: The three modes, or qualities, of material nature: goodness, passion and ignorance.

Hari-bhakti-vilasa: The ritual and devotional practices of the Gaudiya Vaisnava-sampradaya, codified into twenty chapters by Srila Sanatana Gosvami and Srila Gopala Bhatta Gosvami. The work represents extensive scriptural research and includes a Sanskrit commentary written by Srila Sanatana Gosvami called *Dig-darsini Tika*.

Jiva Gosvami: One of the Six Gosvamis of Vrndavana and the nephew of Rupa and Sanatana Gosvamis. His father, Anupama, died when the boy was very young. He grew up absorbed in the worship of Krishna and Balarama. Lord Caitanya instructed him in a dream to proceed to Navadvipa, and there he toured that sacred place in the association of Sri Nityananda Prabhu. He then went to Benares to study Sanskrit, and from there to Vrndavana to be under the shelter of his uncles. He became a disciple of Rupa Gosvami and wrote eighteen major works on Vaisnava philosophy, comprising more than 400,000 verses. He is considered by many philosophers and Sanskritists to be the greatest scholar who ever lived.

Kali: The personification of the Age of Quarrel appearing in the form of a *sudra* (low class man) in the dress of a royal king.

Kali-yuga: The "Age of Quarrel and Hypocrisy." The fourth and last age in the cycle of four ages. This is the present age in which we are now living. It began 5,000 years ago and lasts for a total of 432,000 years. It is characterized by irreligious practice and stringent material miseries.

Karma: Material action performed according to scriptural regulations; Action pertaining to the development of the material body; Any material action which will incur a subsequent reaction; The material reaction one incurs due to fruitive activities; This Sanskrit word means 'action' or, more specifically, any material action that brings a reaction binding us to the material world. According to the law of *karma*, if we cause pain and suffering to other living beings, we must endure pain and suffering in return.

Kauravas: The descendents of King Kuru who fought against the Pandavas in the Battle of Kuruksetra.

Krishna: A confidential name for God, the Supreme Personality of Godhead, Who is the source of all things; He is referred to in various traditions as Allah, Jehovah, Lord, Supreme, etc.

Kuruksetra: A holy place due to the penances of King Kuru. It was here that the great *Mahabharata* war was fought, situated about ninety miles north of New Delhi, where Lord Krishna spoke the *Bhagavad-gita* to Arjuna five thousand years ago. It is a place of pilgrimage.

Madhvacarya: A great thirteenth-century Vaisnava spiritual master, who preached the theistic philosophy of pure dualism. The founder of the *dvaita* school of *Vedanta* philosophy. He wrote a number of works that refuted the impersonal philosophy of Sankaracarya. He appeared in the 13th century in Udipi, in South India. He took *sannyasa* at the age of twelve, traveled all over India and had the personal association of Srila Vyasadeva in the Himalayan abode of Badarikashrama and presented his commentary on *Bhagavad-gita* before that venerable sage. He was very powerful both physically and intellectually, and was considered to be an incarnation of Vayu, the wind god.

Maitreya Muni: The great sage who spoke *Srimad-Bhagavatam* to Vidura and who gave advice to the Pandavas during their exile in the forest. He cursed Duryodhana that Bhima would fulfill his vow.

Mahabharata: An ancient, Sanskrit, epic history of Bharata, or India composed by Krishna Dvaipayana Vyasadeva, the literary incarnation of Godhead, in 100,000 verses. The essence of all Vedic philosophy, the *Bhagavad-gita*, is a part of this great work. *Mahabharata* is a history of the earth from its creation to the great Kuruksetra war fought between the Kuru and Pandava factions of the Kaurava dynasty, which took place about five thousand years ago. The battle was waged to determine who would be the emperor of the world: the saintly Yudhisthira, a Vaisnava king, or the evil-minded Duryodhana, the son of Dhritarastra.

Maharaja: Literally means "great king."

Mantra: (*ma*: mind + *tra*: deliverance) A pure sound vibration which, when repeated over and over, delivers the mind from its material inclinations and illusion. A transcendental sound or Vedic hymn, a prayer or chant.

Manu-samhita: The scriptural law book for mankind, written by Manu, the administrative demigod and father of mankind.

Naimisaranya: A sacred forest in central India where the eighteen Puranas were spoken and which is said to be the hub of the universe.

Nanda Maharaja: The king of the cowherd men of Vrndavana, Vraja, foster father of Lord Krishna.

Nimbarkacarya: Great Vaisnava saint and spiritual master in the line of the Kumara-sampradaya.

Pandavas: The five pious *ksatriya* brothers Yudhisthira, Bhima, Arjuna, Nakula and Sahadeva. They were intimate friends of Lord Krishna's and inherited the leadership of the world upon their victory over the Kurus in the Battle of Kuruksetra.

Pandita: A learned scholar.

Pariksit: The son of Abhimanyu and grandson of Arjuna. He was named Pariksit, meaning 'the examiner,' as the Brahmins said he would come to examine all men in his search for the Supreme Lord, whom he saw while he was still an embryo in his mother's womb. When the Pandavas retired from kingly life, he was crowned king of the entire world. He was later cursed to die by an immature *brahmana* boy. He heard *Srimad-Bhagavatam* from Sukadeva Gosvami, and thus attained perfection.

Parampara: The disciplic succession through which spiritual knowledge is transmitted by bona fide spiritual masters.

Prithu Maharaja: An empowered incarnation of Lord Krishna who demonstrated how to be an ideal ruler.

Puranas: The eighteen major and eighteen minor ancient Vedic literatures compiled about five thousand years ago in India by Srila Vyasadeva. These are histories of this and other planets; literatures supplementary to the *Vedas*, discussing such topics as the creation of the universe, incarnations of the Supreme Lord and demigods, and the history of dynasties of saintly kings. The eighteen principal Puranas discuss ten primary subject matters: 1) the primary creation, 2) the secondary creation, 3) the planetary systems, 4) protection and maintenance by the *avataras*, 5) the Manus 6) dynasties of great kings, 7) noble character and activities of great kings, 8) dissolution of the universe and liberation of the living entity, 9) the *jiva* (the spirit soul), 10) the Supreme Lord.

Rajarsi: A great saintly king.

Ramacandra: The eighteenth incarnation of the Supreme Personality of Godhead and the killer of the ten-headed demon King Ravana. Rama was exiled to the forest on the order of His father, King Dasaratha. His wife Sita was kidnapped by Ravana, but by employing a huge army of monkeys, who were the powerful and intelligent offspring of demigods, He regained his wife in battle, and eventually His ancestral kingdom as well. This great epic is recounted in Valmiki's *Ramayana*.

Ramanujacarya: A great eleventh-century Vaisnava spiritual master of the Sri-sampradaya.

Ramayana: The original epic history about Lord Ramacandra and Sita, written by Valmiki Muni.

Rupa Gosvami: Chief of the six great spiritual master Gosvamis of Vrndavana who were authorized by Lord Caitanya Mahaprabhu to establish and distribute the philosophy of Krishna consciousness. He extensively researched the scriptures and established the philosophy taught by Lord Caitanya on an unshakable foundation. Thus Gaudiya Vaisnavas are known as *Rupanugas*, followers of Rupa Gosvami.

Sadhu: A saint or God-conscious devotee, or Vaisnava. A wandering holy man.

Sampradaya: A disciplic succession of spiritual masters, along with the followers in that tradition, through which spiritual knowledge is transmitted.

Sanat-Kumara: One of the four *kumaras* (sages in the form of young children) who are sons of Lord Brahma. He is the head of the *kumara-sampradaya*, which is one of the four Vaisnava systems of disciplic succession.

Sankaracarya: An incarnation of Lord Siva who appeared in South India at the end of the 7th century A.D. to re-establish the authority of the Vedic scriptures. He was a philosopher and lived about three hundred years before Ramanuja. He lived at a time when India was under the sway of Buddhism, whose tenets deny the authority of the *Vedas*. He took *sannyasa* at a very tender age and wrote commentaries establishing an impersonal philosophy similar to Buddhism, substituting Brahman (Spirit) for the void. He traveled all over India defeating the great scholars of the day and converting them to his doctrine of Mayavada, the *advaita* (non-dualism) interpretation of the Upanishads and Vedanta. He left the world at the age of thirty-three.

Sannyasa: Renounced life; the fourth order of Vedic spiritual life.

Sanskrit: The oldest language in the world. The *Vedas*, or India's holy scriptures, are written in Sanskrit.

Siksamrta: A book by Srila Bhaktivinoda Thakur; literally means "nectarean teachings."

Siksastaka: Eight verses by Lord Caitanya Mahaprabhu glorifying the chanting of the Lord's holy name.

Sri Tattva-sandarbha: A work written by Jiva Gosvami wherein it is explained that *Srimad-Bhagavatam* is the most authoritative evidence directly pointing to the Absolute Truth.

Srila Prabhupada: (1896-1977) His Divine Grace A.C. Bhaktivedanta Swami Prabhupada. Tenth-generation disciple from Caitanya Mahaprabhu. The founder-*acarya*, spiritual master of the largest present-day branch of the Gaudiya Math in the west (ISKCON). Srila Prabhupada was the widely-acclaimed author of more than seventy books on the science of pure *bhakti-yoga*, unalloyed God consciousness. His major works are annotated English translations of the *Srimad-Bhagavatam*, the *Sri Caitanya-caritamrta* and the *Bhagavad-gita: As It Is*. He was one of the world's most distinguished teachers of Vedic religion and thought. Srila Prabhupada was a fully God-conscious saint who had perfect realization of the Vedic scriptures. He worked incessantly to spread God consciousness all over the world. He guided his society and saw it grow to a worldwide confederation of hundreds of ashrams, schools, temples, institutes and farm communities.

Srimad-Bhagavatam: The *Bhagavata Purana*; foremost of the eighteen *Puranas*, the complete science of God that establishes the supreme position of Lord Krishna. It was glorified by Sri Caitanya Mahaprabhu as the *amalam* *puranam*, "the purest *Purana*." It was written by Srila Vyasadeva as his commentary on the *Vedanta-sutra*, and it deals exclusively with topics concerning the Supreme Personality of Godhead (Lord Krishna) and His devotees.

Sukadeva Gosvami: An exalted devotee who recited the *Srimad-Bhagavatam* to King Pariksit during the last seven days of the King's life.

Suta Gosvami: The son of Romaharsana. He was the great sage who related the discourse between King Pariksit and Sukadeva Gosvami, which forms the basis of the *Srimad-Bhagavatam*.

Ugrasena: The king of the Yadus and the father of Kamsa.

Uttanapada: The king who was a son of Svayambhuva Manu and the father of King Dhruva.

Vaisnava: A devotee of the Supreme Lord. Such devotees honor all bona fide religions and saints and recognize that there is one Supreme God who sends various representatives according to time and place.

Vanaras: A race of gorillas that existed during the time of Lord Ramacandra.

Varnasrama-dharma: The system of four social (*varna*) and four spiritual (*ashrama*) orders established in the Vedic scriptures and discussed by Krishna in the *Bhagavad-gita*. This system is to help people become more God-conscious while honoring their natural propensities.

Vedanta-sutra: Srila Vyasadeva's conclusive summary of Vedic philosophical knowledge. Written in brief codes, it shows Krishna as the goal.

Vedas: The original revealed scriptures, first spoken by Lord Krishna.

Vedic: Pertaining to a culture in which all aspects of human life are under the guidance of the *Vedas*.

Vena: The demoniac son of King Anga and father of King Prithu; he was a sinful king who had to be dethroned by the *brahmanas*.

Vidura: The son of Vyasadeva by a maidservant of Ambalika and the half brother of Dhritarastra. He was an incarnation of the great devotee *mahajana* Yamaraja, and an uncle of the Pandavas. A great devotee of Krishna who inquired and heard from Maitreya Muni, as narrated in *Srimad-Bhagavatam*. He was cursed to become a *sudra* by Mandavya Muni. He was constantly trying to restrain Dhritarastra from mistreating the Pandavas. In the end when Dhritarastra lost everything, Vidura was able to deliver his brother to the path of self-realization.

Vrindavana: Krishna's eternal abode, where He fully manifests His quality of sweetness. Also the name of the village on Earth in which He enacted His childhood pastimes five thousand years ago.

Vyasadeva: The sage who gave the *Vedas*, *Puranas*, *Vedanta-sutra* and *Mahabharata* to mankind. Born from the union of Parasara Rishi and Satyavati, he is known as Dwaipayana because he was born on an island. He compiled the *Vedas* and is said to be an empowered incarnation of Visnu. His son's name is Sukadeva, the famous reciter of the *Srimad-Bhagavatam* (*Bhagavata Purana*).

Yajna: A Vedic sacrifice.

Yamaraja: The demigod of death, who passes judgment at the time of death. He is the son of the sun-god and the brother of the sacred river Yamuna.

Yamuna: The sacred river where Krishna performed many pastimes. One of the holy rivers in India flowing through Vrindavana. It is here that Lord Krishna sported as a child.

Yoga: A spiritual discipline meant for linking one's consciousness with the Supreme Lord, Krishna.

Yudhisthira: The eldest of the Pandavas in the *Mahabharata*, and the son of Dharmaraja or Yamaraja, the god of death. Famous for his adherence to virtue and truth, he is also known as Dharmaraja, as well as Ajatashatru, which means "one who has no enemies." It was the dispute over his succession to the throne in India that led to the Battle of Kuruksetra; he ruled the earth for thirty-six years after the Kuruksetra war and was succeeded by Pariksit.

BIBLIOGRAPHY

Blanchard, Ken. *The Heart of a Leader*. Guildford, Surrey, UK: Eagle, Inter Publishing Services, 1999.

Block, Peter. *Stewardship*. San Francisco: Berrett-Koehler Publishers, 1993.

Cashman, Kevin. *Leadership from the Inside Out*. Provo, Utah: Executive Excellence Publishing, 1998.

Chakraborty. *Management by Values*. Delhi, India: Oxford University Press, 1995.

Collins & Porras. *Built to Last: Successful Habits of Visionary Companies*. New York: Harper Business, 1994.

Covey, Stephen. *The Seven Habits of Highly Effective People*. New York: Fireside, Simon & Schuster, 1990.

———. *Principle Centered Leadership*. New York: Fireside, Simon & Schuster, 1992.

Davidson, Gordon. *Visionary Voices: Leadership for a New Era; Vol. 1, No.2*. Washington DC: The Center for Visionary Leadership, 1997.

Gibson, Rowan. *Rethinking the Future*. London: Nicholas Brealey Publishing, 1998.

Goldsmith, Marshall; Lyons, Laurence; Freas, Alyssa. *Coaching For Leadership*. San Francisco: Jossey-Bass/Pfeiffer, 2000.

Greenleaf, Robert K. *Servant Leadership*. New York: Paulist Press, 1977.

Greenleaf, Robert K. *The Leadership Crisis*. Indianapolis, IN: The Greenleaf Center for Servant-Leadership, 1986.

Hawley, Jack. *Reawakening the Spirit in Work*. San Francisco: Berrett-Koehler Publishers, 1993.

Hesselbein, F.; Goldsmith, M.; Beckhard, R. *The Leader of the Future*. San Francisco: Jossey-Bass Publishers, 1996.

Josephson, M. & Hanson, W., ed.; *The Power of Character*. San Francisco, Jossey-Bass, 1998

Lee, Blaine. *The Power Principle*. New York: Fireside, Simon & Schuster, 1997.

Maslow, Abraham. *Toward a Psychology of Being*. New York: Van Nostrand Reinhold, 1968

Maxwell, John. *Developing the Leaders Around You*. Nashville, Tenn.: T. Nelson, 1995

McLaughlin & Davidson. *Spiritual Politics*. New York: Ballantine Books, 1994.

Mishra, B.B. *Polity in the Agni Purana*. Calcutta, India: Calcutta Oriental Press, 1965.

Mitroff & Denton. *A Spiritual Audit of Corporate America*. San Francisco: Jossey-Bass Publishers, 1999.

Nair, Keshavan. *A Higher Standard of Leadership*. San Francisco: Berrett-Koehler Publishers, 1994.

Ornish, Dean. *Love and Survival*. New York: Harper Collins Publishers, 1998.

Palmer, Parker J. *Leading from Within: Reflections on Spirituality and Leadership*. Indiana Office for Campus Ministries, March 1990.

Patterson & Kim. *The Day America Told the Truth*. New York: Prentice Hall Press, 1991

Rifkin, Jeremy. *The Age of Access*. New York: Tarcher/Putnam, 2000.

Schemm, Peter R. *Love: Impact on Physical and Mental Health*. Kearney, NE: Morris Publishing, 1996.

Shelton, Ken. *Executive Excellence, Vol.16, No.8*. Provo, Utah: Executive Excellence Publishing, 1999.

———. *Beyond Counterfeit Leadership*. Provo, Utah: Executive Excellence Publishing, 1997.

Spears, Larry C. *Insights on Leadership*. New York: John Wiley & Sons, 1998.

———. *Reflections on Leadership*. New York: John Wiley & Sons, 1995.

Swami, B.T. *Leadership for an Age of Higher Consciousness*. Washington DC: Harinama Press, 1996.

———. *Spiritual Warrior II: Transforming Lust into Love*. Washington DC: Harinama Press, 1998

———. *Spiritual Warrior III: Solace for the Heart in Difficult Times*. Washington DC: Harinama Press, 2000

Swami Prabhupada, A.C. Bhaktivedanta. *Bhagavad-gita: As It Is*. Victoria, Australia: Bhaktivedanta Book Trust, 1993.

———. *Srimad Bhagavatam*. Los Angeles: Bhaktivedanta Book Trust, 1994.

Tulgan, Bruce. *Managing Generation X*. New York: W.W. Norton & Company, Inc., 2000.

Wheatley, Margaret J. *Leadership and the New Science*. San Francisco: Berrett-Koehler Publishers, 1992.

Whitty, Michael D. & Biberman, Jerry (Eds.). *Work and Spirit*. University of Scranton Press, 2000.

Williamson, Marianne. *The Healing of America*. New York: Simon & Schuster, 1997.

ABOUT THE AUTHOR

Bhakti Tīrtha Swami was born John E. Favors in a pious, God-fearing family. As a child evangelist, he appeared regularly on television, and as a young man, he was a leader in Dr. Martin Luther King, Jr.'s civil rights movement. At Princeton University, he became president of the student council and also served as chairman of the Third World Coalition. Although his main degree is in psychology, he has received accolades in many other fields, including politics, African studies, and international law.

Bhakti Tīrtha Swami's books are used as reference texts in universities and leadership organizations throughout the world. Many of his books have been printed in English, German, French, Spanish, Portuguese, Macedonian, Croatian, Russian, Hebrew, Slovenian, Balinese, and Italian.

His Holiness has served as assistant coordinator for penal reform programs in the State of New Jersey, Office of the Public Defender, and as a director of several drug abuse clinics in the United States. In addition, he has been a special consultant for Educational Testing Services in the U.S.A. and has managed campaigns for politicians. Bhakti Tīrtha Swami gained international recognition as a representative of the Bhaktivedanta Book Trust, particularly for his outstanding work with scholars in the former communist countries of Eastern Europe.

Bhakti Tīrtha Swami directly oversaw projects in the United States (particularly Washington D.C., Potomac, Maryland, Detroit, Pennsylvania, West Virginia), West Africa, South Africa, Switzerland, France, Croatia, and Bosnia. He also served as the director of the American Federation of Vaisnava Colleges and Schools.

In the United States, Bhakti Tīrtha Swami was the founder and director of the Institute for Applied Spiritual Technology, director of the International Committee for Urban Spiritual Development, and one of the international coordinators of the Seventh Pan African Congress. Reflecting his wide range of interests, he was also a member of the Institute for Noetic Sciences, the Center for Defense Information, the United Nations Association for America, the National Peace Institute Foundation, the World Future Society, and the Global Forum of Spiritual and Parliamentary Leaders.

A specialist in international relations and conflict resolution, Bhakti Tīrtha Swami constantly traveled around the world and had become a spiritual consultant to many high-ranking members of the United Nations, to various celebrities, and to several chiefs, kings, and high court justices. In 1990, His Holi- ness was coronated as a high chief in Warri, Nigeria in recognition for his outstanding work in Africa and the world. In recent years, he met several times with then-President Nelson Mandela of South Africa to share visions and strategies for world peace.

In addition to encouraging self-sufficiency through the development of schools, clinics, farm projects, and cottage industries, Bhakti Tīrtha Swami conducted seminars and workshops on principle-centered leadership, spiritual development, interpersonal relationships, stress and time management, and other pertinent topics. He was also widely acknowledged as a viable participant in the resolution of global conflict.

On August 5, 2004, Bhakti Tīrtha Swami was diagnosed with melanoma cancer in his left foot. Although he made every effort to treat his condition, the cancer continued to spread, leading His Holiness to teach the most important lesson—how to die. During the time after his diagnosis, he gave numerous lectures on the topic and completed a book of meditations, The Beggar IV: Die Before Dying, also dedicated to this same topic. Almost a year later, on June 27, 2005, His Holiness departed from this world, surrounded by loving friends, relatives, and disciples.

Although His Holiness Bhakti Tīrtha Swami has seemingly gone, he actually left behind him a powerful legacy that will continue to live on through his students and well-wishers, and especially through his books. Numerous lectures, seminars, and workshops wait in the archives for Hari-Nama Press to transcribe and to then publish in future books. B.T. Swami's teachings will undoubtedly continue through these unique books and through the lives of those who imbibe his message.

BOOKS FROM HARI-NAMA PRESS

Leadership for an Age of Higher Consciousness I: Administration from a Metaphysical Perspective

Leadership for an Age of Higher Consciousness II: Ancient Wisdom for Modern Times

Spiritual Warrior I: Uncovering Spiritual Truths in Psychic Phenomena

Spiritual Warrior II: Transforming Lust into Love

Spiritual Warrior III: Solace for the Heart in Difficult Times

Spiritual Warrior IV: Conquering the Enemies of the Mind

Spiritual Warrior V: Making the Mind Your Best Friend

Spiritual Warrior VI: Beyond Fanaticism, Terrorism, and War: Discover the Peace Solution

Reflections on Sacred Teachings I: Sri Siksastaka

Reflections on Sacred Teachings II: Madhurya-Kadambini

Reflections on Sacred Teachings III: Harinama Cintamani

Reflections on Sacred Teachings IV: Sri Isopanisad

Reflections on Sacred Teachings V: Srila Bhaktisiddhanta's Sixty-four Principles for Community

Reflections on Sacred Teachings VI: Radha-Sunya: Missing Mercy

The Beggar I: Meditations and Prayers on the Supreme Lord

The Beggar II: Crying Out for the Mercy

The Beggar III: False Ego: The Greatest Enemy of the Spiritual Leader

The Beggar IV: Die Before Dying

Surrender: The Key to Eternal Life

Black Lotus: The Spiritual Journey of an Urban Mystic

www.ingramcontent.com/pod-product-compliance
Lightning Source LLC
Chambersburg PA
CBHW052342220526
45465CB00003BA/921